BLAH TO BLING

BLING

Living the Exceptional Life

Venus Stark

Venus Stark

Published byVenus Stark

Requests for permission to make copies of any part of this work can be made to:

Venus Stark

345 Lakeview Dr.

Grantsville Md 21536

Table of Contents

Introduction

What Is Blah to Bling

"Putting the 'life' back into 'life' is about passion."

Bling is passion, excitement, purpose, and meaning. It is living an Exceptional life full of energy, vigor, and fulfillment, waking up each morning thrilled to start your day.

Blah is simply going through the motions of everyday life with no passion or interest. It's giving up, it's settling, it is life without excitement.

Bling is snapping yourself out of the delusions that say, "I can't, I'm afraid, I don't know how," and stepping through the door of your life. Bling is announcing, "No more excuses, no more settling. I have control over my life, no one and nothing else does. I will give everything my all, I have the power to change, and I choose to live my life with passion."

Blah is being on the outside looking in to a life you only dream of. Picture yourself window shopping, dreaming of the life that could have been. Visions of regret, guilt, missed opportunity, what ifs, and should haves flash through your mind. You shake your head to wake yourself out of a world of delusion, telling yourself it was only a dream.

Bling is making the choice to live an Exceptional life, one full of excitement and passion. This will bring fulfillment to your life and empower you to be the person you long to be, not the person someone else wishes you to be. You must demand it of yourself—no one else will.

Blah is allowing yourself to fall into a mundane existence, doing only what you must, telling yourself it is OK because that is what everyone else is doing. Blah is just getting through life, giving up on what is important to you, and simply allowing life to happen as it may.

Bling is confidence. Passion is what builds your confidence, which will lead you to belief in yourself and which will fuel the fire of your passions to an even higher level.

Blah is insecurity and low self-esteem.

Bling is the freedom to choose your destiny gained by giving everything your all and living a passionate life.

Blah is the prison of fear, doubt, guilt, and regret created by settling for less and giving up on what was important to you.

Bling is about creating balance by following your passions. You can only be your best in all you do if you are excited. Passion is a fire that will spread to all areas of your life, not just a few. Living an Exceptional life begins with balance—you will have to settle for less somewhere in your life if you don't.

Blah To Bling

Blah is a lopsided life. You may excel in some areas, giving them all you've got, but shortcut others.

Bling is striving to be your best.

Blah is settling for being around others who do not.

Bling is not giving up your time with those you care about.

Blah is buying gifts to make up for your time. There is no substitute for your love and attention.

Bling is taking time to plan and prepare healthy meals, so you can perform at your best.

Blah is allowing your career to keep you so busy that fast food has become the standard meal, and settling for less than your best health.

Bling is finding pleasure in the small sacrifices to your success and pushing through to the rewards.

Blah is giving in to the pain of the sacrifices needed for your success instead of enduring.

If you are not willing to make the effort to be Exceptional (Bling), you will have to settle for the acceptable (Blah).

Do you choose *Blah* or *Bling*?

What This Book Will Do for You

Our deepest fear is that we are not good enough. We ask ourselves, "Who am I to be brilliant, gorgeous, successful, and fabulous?" What you need to ask yourself instead is, "Who am I not to be those things?"

This book will forever change your life, mindset, health, and results because of the transformation you will go through after gaining the knowledge within. Understand that I cannot change you—only you can choose to do that. I can only give you the insights, tools, and guidance to change where you are now to where you want to go. It is your journey, not mine; it is what is important to you, not to me or anyone else.

You will discover why giving up on your passions has led you to give up on a life of excitement.

You will realize that confidence is gained through your passions, because excitement is what makes us strive to be our best. Confidence builds belief in yourself and it is your belief that fuels the intensity of your passion and excitement for an Exceptional life.

You will learn to master the mindsets, traits, and habits of excellence, which will put Bling in your life. Understand that confident people have their struggles too; being Exceptional is nothing more than doing everything with passion. You will have a sense of fulfillment because at the end of the day you know you have done your best.

You will realize you have the power within you to be what you want, to get what you desire, and to accomplish whatever you are striving for. It is much easier than you think to possess self-confidence. You simply develop it one day, choice, habit, and thought at a time through consistent effort. Yes, I said effort—first you need to face the reality that you are going to have to make some changes. The definition of insanity is doing the same things over and over and expecting different results. Sorry, it just doesn't work that way.

You will understand that to develop confidence, you must decide that you are willing to make some changes in your life that will forever change your results. Now, maybe some of you are thinking, "I don't need to make changes, I am happy with my current results." If so, put the book down and walk away. However, if you are reading this, I believe inside you know that you are not happy with your current circumstances. Accept the fact that you are tired of feeling insecure, not believing in yourself, and bouncing through life with little or no direction. Say it with me: "I can change anything in my life the minute I decide to."

You will wake up every day with excitement to start your day. You'll no longer carry the baggage of the internal feelings of self-defeat, and you will never go back to a life of settling. Once you come out of the forest of delusion and see the light of a life filled with purpose and meaning, you will want to develop, maintain, and grow your new habits of freedom. Life was meant to be cherished and lived every day, not to be something you endure and wait patiently through, hoping to arrive safely at death.

You will learn how to "Believe in Yourself." It takes the right tools, habits, and learning to think—really think, not just let your thoughts run randomly. It can be done and must be done to succeed; no one can motivate you until you believe. You will have to be your own coach, mentor, judge, and jury because no one knows what is going on in your mind.

Unless you share your thoughts with someone you trust, and I highly recommend you do, you will not be able to receive support from others. Having someone who will snap you back into reality is essential. It's easy to convince yourself that you are doing what you need to do and thinking what you need to think, but when you say the lies you are telling yourself out loud, they are exposed for what they really are. This is OK because you cannot turn it around until you catch yourself, and that is the trick to achieving belief in yourself: stopping disbelief dead in its tracks.

I always said my mantra was "BELIEVE," but I didn't really understand why. I took it as "Believe in God," or in a purpose or just *believe*. I said it, but deep down I was so full of self-doubt that I was the biggest hypocrite of them all. Then, like a lightning bolt, I realized that everything—I mean everything—starts with believing in yourself. That's the true key to happiness and success. We can only be our best selves when we feel comfortable with who we are—and how can we possibly do that if we don't believe in ourselves?

You will discover the greatest gift you have been given is your power to choose: you never have to settle for circumstances, results, or situations. You have, at any given time, the power to choose what you want, what you don't want, how you will react to something, your attitude, your perception, and any action you will take or not take. Self-confidence is the driving force of your power; it is the bridge between being your best, going the extra mile, doing all that you can, and settling for less than your best. Everything counts—every action, thought, and choice counts. Your choices are all rooted in your beliefs that is why believing in yourself is crucial, the choices you make are usually based on your beliefs.

You will see it is easy to follow the tribe, go with the flow, not make any waves. But ask yourself: Am I tired of being imprisoned by fear, doubt, or embarrassment? Is my life going the direction I want or is it going where someone or something else is pushing me? Remember the only opinion that matters is the one in the mirror. Making no choice is a choice in itself; if you do not choose, some other force will choose for you. Taking the easy way out or the path of least resistance does not usually lead anywhere you want to go. You must choose to do what you know is best, even when you don't want to.

You will realize that if you must sacrifice your health, family, or peace of mind to have more luxuries, then they are not truly luxuries. They have control over you and will cause you to settle. This does not mean you should not want and work to have nice things; it simply means the greatest luxury is balance in all that you do.

You will gain the insight that the scariest thing about settling for being less than your best is that you are choosing to not think. If you were truly thinking about what you want, you would never decide to be average. Who wants to be average? You deserve so much more and all you must do is think, decide, and take action.

You will begin your journey to confidence. You will decide to step off the Blah land of despair you are standing on and onto the bridge of confidence. By committing to learning and gaining the insights within this book, you will be led across to the other side, to a life of Bling.

Why You Want Confidence

"Confidence determines our ability."

Normal is not something to aspire to.

You don't wish to be ordinary, but without confidence, that is what you accept.

With confidence, you don't go through life accepting whatever others have told you because you have your own beliefs in your ability to go after what you want.

Confidence makes you feel like you can trust and rely on yourself; there is a connection between who you are and who you wish to be.

Having confidence allows you to make decisions based on what you want, not what others have led you to believe you want. Such as, where you live, who you will marry, what you eat, whether to have children, what career to choose—the list goes on and on.

Having low confidence will affect every area of your life—usually without you even knowing it because it blinds you to the truth.

If there is no other possession in the world you ever have, confidence is the one thing you must strive for. If you wish to live a life of passion, purpose, and fulfillment, you must have confidence. Without it, you will always be the product of outside forces that do not care about you.

Confidence will guide you to fulfill your dreams and desires. It will give you success in all you do, from your health to being you. You are the only one who can decide to not live at surface level, not to be average or mediocre, not to take the easy, comfortable way.

When you have confidence, you make every effort to be your best in all you do, and everything will change in your life. You won't even recognize your surroundings; you will wonder why you have allowed yourself to settle for so long. The truth usually is that you didn't even realize you were doing it.

Your life will have new meaning—you'll wake up excited for the day instead of hitting the snooze alarm.

You will no longer allow outside circumstances to dictate your attitude or allow others' ways of thinking to seep into your head and steal your thoughts.

Your true passions will surface, and your purpose will reveal itself. Confidence makes you want to dig deeper to discover the true riches that can be found when you put in the extra effort. All of these things lie below the surface, and when you are confident you will not choose to live only at surface level.

Have you just accepted your current job, income, home, or life in general because you don't think anything better is possible, you think that you are not good enough or smart enough, or it's just too late now? Is it easier to just settle where you are because outside of that comfort zone, it's scary and too hard?

Life is not lived in a state of comfort; nothing grows or improves there. The comfort zone is stagnant, with no rewards or fulfillment. If you think standing still is safer, you are wrong, because there is no such thing—we are either moving forward or backward. The world is ever evolving and moving, and life does not stand still. You either roll with it, change, and create your future, or fall behind, get run over, and get left in the past. You know that is not what you want, but you don't know how to change it, or create the change you want to see happen. Confidence: that is the secret to changing your life and results from an acceptable existence to an Exceptional one.

When you have confidence, you will realize that the people you view as confident were in your shoes once— you are not alone. Some still struggle with their self-esteem, body image, and confidence. They were not born with confidence; they built it one choice, thought, habit, and step at a time, and so can you.

Confidence helps you conquer your greatest fears and learn how to build an ironclad wall of courage around yourself to protect you from the biggest naysayer— yourself! I learned through many failures, heartaches, and trials; I have studied and continue to grow and learn from the most confident, successful people in all walks of life.

—

Section 1: Mindsets

How You Think Will Determine Your Life

Your mindset is how you perceive yourself, your circumstances, the results you get, the world, and everyone around you, so you can see why it is so important to your success. How you think about things determines your life. The confident, Exceptional people have a different mindset than the ordinary thinkers. To change the trajectory of your life, you need to adopt a new way of thinking. This will determine your traits and habits.

Here's an example. When my niece was heading off to college, she was excited but scared and worried too, of course. She said to me, "It's going to be hard, I'm going to be stressed, and I don't know if I can succeed."

I quickly stopped her in her tracks. I told her to stop focusing on those things, because what you are thinking about is what you're drawn toward. I explained that what we focus on becomes our thoughts and our thoughts become our reality. She wanted to be a pharmacist and her dream car was a Range Rover, so I told her that when fear, doubt, worry, stress, and difficult times faced her, she should focus on driving her Range Rover to her pharmacy, thinking about how great it will feel. I explained if she kept her mindset focused on that, everything else would only be background noise.

Blah To Bling

Putting the Bling in your life starts with how you perceive the events and people around you—life is all a perception.

Live Life with Passion

"If you are working on something exciting that you really care about, you don't have to be pushed. The vision pulls you."

Your chances of success in any endeavor are far greater if you enjoy what you are doing. Passion creates enthusiasm, which is 90% an inside game. Passion gives you purpose and self-confidence and motivates you. There is not a single recipe to success, but there is one essential ingredient—passion. Bling is living a life of passion, doing the things you enjoy and love, and helping others. A passionate life is fulfilling and empowering and keeps you moving forward with zest. It's living and creating one dream to another.

Passion is leaving work early, getting up early on Saturday morning, and getting home late so you can coach Little League because you love helping the kids. You may even have to work overtime another day to make up for it. However, the feeling you get doing this makes your life have purpose.

Passion is cooking even if you are alone because you love how it makes you feel.

Passion is putting hours of work into a project that will bring you nothing more than fulfillment. It may cost you money, no one may ever appreciate it, and you may even face ridicule, but it excites you.

Blah is settling for what life hands you. Life is too short, so begin today. Don't tell yourself that same old lie, "I will begin tomorrow." It is never too late to reinvent yourself. You can begin living your life with passion at any time you choose. That is what it is all about: filling your days with what makes you happy, not just going through the motions. Life is not about living paycheck to paycheck, it is about happiness, fulfillment, and joy.

Passion is energy. Feel the power that comes from focusing on what excites you.

Never give up on your passions; they are what make you who you are. Never allow others' opinions to keep you from your passion. Passion is what lights your soul, what gives you reasons to leap forward with courage, your very reason for living. When you are passionate about something, it makes you dynamic and magnetic and brings out the best in you. The more you let your natural interests lead you, the more confident and relaxed you will feel.

Blah to Bling example: Tony loved to cook. He loved looking at cookbooks for inspiration, creating exciting menus, and entertaining. Life got busy, others made negative comments about some of his creations, and people asked him, "Why waste your time with that? It is easier to go out to eat." He soon allowed himself to follow the tribe and he started eating out, telling himself, "You are just too busy for that."

Before he knew it, he was going through the motions of day-to-day life with no passion, only the thought of getting by. He didn't understand why he had no real interest in anything anymore—he had a good life, friends, family, and a home and was paying his bills on time, but he just seemed to be Blah.

One day, he was walking past a newsstand when he spotted a cooking magazine. He stopped and glanced through it. All at once, he felt excitement as he looked at the beautiful dishes. He picked out one that he liked, bought the magazine, and was off to the grocery store. He went home and prepared a wonderful, healthy meal for his wife. She was shocked—not that he had cooked, but at the passion in his eyes as he served dinner and talked about how he had prepared it. He talked about some other great ideas he had for the next day and the next and how he was thinking about a get-together for the weekend so he could try out some other recipes.

Tony blew the dust off of his cooking utensils, cookbooks, and skills and went back to doing what made him passionate. Even if he was too busy to cook some nights, he vowed to never fall back into the rut of not doing what he truly loved and gave him purpose.

Add the Bling action step: Write down at least seven things that excite you, that really get you going, and then commit to start doing at least one of them today, not tomorrow.

Bling is choosing to go after your dreams, discovering yourself and your gifts, and sharing them with the

world. Live a life of excitement, enthusiasm, and passion!

Blah is settling for what is easy instead of finding your passion and purpose.

I Believe in Me

"There is more to you than you know. If you can realize it, you will not be willing to settle for less than you deserve."

I believe. I will conquer.

The greatest desire of all is to believe in ourselves. To have faith in our abilities, a feeling of true self-appreciation, to be comfortable in our own skin. To truly love who we are and have the courage to be our genuine selves. Believing in yourself is so important because it is your opinion of yourself that determines what will happen in your life. You can study, work your butt off, and take action, but if in your mind and heart you do not believe it is possible, it will not happen. You will constantly be fighting the naysayers within, and they are the most destructive of all enemies. You will argue with others who say things you don't like and refuse to listen to them, but you can never escape the broken record in your head until you decide you are done listening to it and throw it away for good. This is not easy and is a skill you will have to develop and practice every minute of your day if you wish to escape the grip of defeat.

I was watching a moth that had gotten into my home. For the first hour or so it continued to bang against the screen. It could see where it wanted to go and had the will to get there, but had no ability to think and make a change. After a few hours, it just sat on the screen with no movement, no more will. It was resigned to just stay there and wait. I thought it was dead, but when I went over to remove it, it was not—well, not physically, at least. Mentally, it was. I considering flushing it and putting it out of its misery because it would only end up against another screen soon, but instead decided to give it another chance. I opened the screen, and off it flew to its next obstacle. The difference between you and that moth is you *do* have the ability to think, to change your direction, to make a plan for success.

We allow ourselves to act in the same way as the moth: we have a dream or desire to achieve something, but as soon as we hit our screen, the disbelief in our minds, we stop dead and resolve to just exist instead. "What's the point anyway?" we think. "I will never be able to have what I want, so why try?"

This is very sad, and you may be thinking, "That's not me, I would never settle if I thought I could have more." However, your thoughts are like subway cars flashing by: you allow ideas to go by without ever stopping long enough to consider the possibilities of those thoughts. You think you can have more or be more but in a flash the thought is gone. The bad thoughts seem to come to a screeching stop, letting you dwell on them. Since you are at a standstill with negative thoughts, you don't move forward to the positive, productive thoughts you should be focusing on.

If you were on a trip and your navigation said you were going the wrong way and you need to make a U-turn, you would do that right away. Well, maybe not until she warns you again, but you certainly wouldn't continue heading where you don't want to go. I mean, really, who wants to be lost, delayed, or sidetracked from their destination? So why then do you ignore all the signs in your life telling you that you are heading the wrong way down a one-way street? You are the result of your choices and can simply change the direction of your life any time you choose, but you don't. Why? Because you don't truly believe that you can. In your mind, you don't believe you can change. You believe only the other guy can be rich, or be successful, or have a beautiful home, a new car, or a boat. You simply do not believe it is possible for you; you allow self-doubt, fear, and procrastination to paralyze you, and there you sit like the moth on the screen. Feeling like there is no hope for you, what is the point I wasn't blessed like the others.

Most believe you are born with confidence, when in fact it is developed; it is a relationship with yourself, and like all relationships, it takes nurturing. Can you image having a best friend you didn't trust or believe in, that you couldn't count on when you needed them most? My guess is you wouldn't keep that friend around for long. To conquer yourself, you must first believe that you can.

All of us can develop belief. History proves time and time again that the greatest achievements were not accomplished by the most talented, but by those who were willing to take on risks and challenges and see them through.

Bob Proctor, a very successful, Exceptional businessman is a perfect example. He never went to college, and worked an average job with no special skills or talents. However, he had a dream to build a business traveling the world helping others improve their lives.

He began to study from good books, associated himself with mentors that could guide him, and most of all developed belief in himself. He is the owner of a multi-million-dollar company, has his own jet, owns a team, employs many people, and travels the world sharing his message. He has changed thousands of lives, all because he chooses to follow his dreams.

He never let the fact that he didn't have the skills or education deter him. Instead he decided to step out of his comfort zone, ignore the naysayers, and never let anyone steal his Bling. He is now 83 years young and continues to thrive and grow because he follows his passion. Every day there are countless talented, educated individuals attempting to build a successful business who fail because they give up at the first sign of struggle.

In the movie *The Blind Side*, Michael Oher is a homeless young man who came from a life of despair. He had no education, knowledge of the game of football, or support of any kind until Leigh Anne Tuohy came into his life. She believed in him until he learned to believe in himself. He did not have a family to support him, most of the time he didn't have a roof over his head or food to eat, and he had a poor academic record. He had to work hard, study to get into college, and learn how to turn his protective instincts into skills to play football. Many prestigious schools heavily recruited him despite his lack of education. He was drafted into the NFL because he persisted. Although he was graced with a guardian angel, Leigh, he himself had to do the work. There are countless athletes with far more education and talent than Michael who never saw their dreams of playing in the NFL realized.

They were only able to succeed by believing. Others can sense when you don't have faith in yourself. If you don't believe in yourself, you will be less effective in everything you do. There will always be a battle going on inside which will always surface in your actions. When you do not believe in yourself, you are constantly judging your thoughts, actions, skills, and abilities, and there is no trust. This leads to not liking or accepting who you truly are.

Having a good relationship with yourself is the first step on the journey to confidence and living an Exceptional life. Confidence starts by learning to believe in yourself and nurturing that relationship, which will lead to loving the unique and genuine person you truly are; love for oneself brings happiness and confidence. Bling begins with believing in you! The greatest courage is to believe in yourself and love who you are. No one is you, and that is your power.

If you were to ask most people who know me, or even if you asked a stranger, they would assume I was a confident woman. On the outside, I strive for that always, but on the inside, there is a huge battle going on. I am constantly fighting to believe in myself. When I confess this truth to others, they laugh. I tell you this not to brag, but to give you hope that you too can own this thing called confidence. I want you to understand it is something that is earned and not given, and with the right tools, you can build yours too.

The thing that you believe in always happens. It is the belief that makes it happen.

You must empower yourself by having the confident belief that anything is possible, because it truly is if you believe. The more you believe in yourself, the greater your accomplishments. You should always look to others for inspiration and guidance, but you are the only one that can truly empower yourself. Before you begin the journey to living an Exceptional life, you must believe it is possible to become confident—without this mindset, you will fail.

Don't fret about how you are going to gain your confidence, just know that you will and begin. Simply work to develop the mindsets, habits, and traits, and implement the strategies into your life. Do not give any thought to the "how." Just conquer them one at a time. Believe!

Add the Bling action step:

Read: *You Were Born Rich* by Bob Proctor

The Magic of Believing by Claude M Bristol

Watch: *The Blind Side*

Bling is to believe beyond your current circumstances to what will be.

Blah is letting the vicious voices inside steal your beliefs.

I Choose to Be the Exception

"You must become the change you wish to see in the world."

If you want a life of fulfillment, happiness, purpose, and no regrets, you must always choose to do things to the best of your ability, and never settle for acceptable. Don't fall victim to just getting things checked off your list; if you are not going to give it your best, don't do it all. Bling is going that extra step, going above and beyond the ordinary, never accepting less than your best. Your rewards in life are in direct proportion to your effort. If you strive to do things just a little better or with more compassion, you invoke good feelings in others. You are not remembered for what you have accomplished, but rather for how you have made others feel.

It is not what we do that counts, it is how we do it.

When you choose to go the extra step, add that special touch, give generously, do the right thing when no one is looking, and give 110% in all you do, you add Bling to your life and everyone around you.

Being the exception is seeing the opportunity for action and taking it. If you accidently knock something over in a store, you pick it up so someone else doesn't have to. Or If you're driving by an elderly person's home and they are

15

sitting on the porch alone, even if you are very busy, you stop to say hello. Or maybe someone is down on their luck and you pay a bill for them without telling them who did it.

Being your best is promising to help with a project. It's doing not just what is needed, but vowing to give it your best effort no matter what.

Adding a special touch is buying a birthday card because it suits that special person, not grabbing one without reading it.

Providing service to others makes a life worth living, but never do so at the expense of yourself. Although is it wonderful to give, remember the speech you get on airplanes: always put your oxygen mask on first before attempting to help others. This is true in all you do—you are of no value to anyone if you don't care for yourself. You can only give your best service to others when you remain true to your principles, values, purpose and goals.

Real satisfaction, genuine growth, and priceless energy come from helping others. Give with selfless passion, knowing they may never be able to repay you. Choose to sow more than you reap. There are more takers than givers; become a giver and watch the rewards multiply in your life.

Blah to Bling example: My dad is the perfect example of being the exception. He is always willing to help everyone, friend or stranger—although there aren't many strangers in my dad's life because he talks to everyone. He worked a full-time job and in the evenings would work

16

many long hours in addition to build his own business. He volunteered with the local fire department and was always there for his family when they needed anything. Even when he was very busy, he never appeared that way: he would stop to assist perfect strangers, do things for others in need, and never accepted a thing for it.

Growing up, I watched him give over ad over again with never a thought to receiving anything in return. I saw many lives touched, and so many smiles and such genuine gratitude from the people he helped. I asked him why he gave so much when many of those people would never repay him, and he said that if you give the best of yourself, it will always come back in some way—maybe not from the ones you gave to, but rewards will always come back. I realized the greatest reward he received was the feeling he got when he gave. My dad understood the concept of paying it forward long before it was a trend or tagline. I will be forever grateful for the wonderful example he set for me and I try my best to do the same.

Add the Bling action step: Begin today to try to be a good example for others to follow in all you do. The next time you are faced with a task, ask yourself, "How could I do it just a little better?" and do it. Don't just do it because you have to or to get it over with. Truly put in the extra effort to make it special.

Bling is giving of yourself freely, going above and beyond your call of duty, and being the difference between acceptable and Exceptional.

Blah is doing only what you feel you must do and nothing more, settling for average.

I Ignore the Insecure Naysayers

"Self-confidence is power."

To believe in yourself, you will need to learn to ignore the naysayers of the world. They are all around you and will destroy your confidence in many sneaky ways. They will say you can't succeed because they fear change, or are afraid that you may get more than them. You wanting to be more threatens their self-esteem.

Insecure people try to build their confidence by putting others down. They think if they make others look or feel bad, they look smarter, more important, or stronger. You can never build your self-worth by degrading others; it can only be built from within. It does not come from the outside world. Exceptional people ignore others who try to put them down because they know their own value and no one can take that from them unless they allow it. You are in control; never put others down to gain your confidence.

Naysayers appear when you get something new you have worked hard for. You are very proud but others around you criticize your choices. Or you put out the effort to make yourself look nice for a party, but all you hear are negative comments. Or you decide to start a new business and you are met with discouraging comments— "You can't do that," "You won't make it," "You are crazy."

Remember, when others are putting you down, it's their insecurities talking. It is actually jealously at work.

Blah to Bling example: Bill worked construction. He put in long hours and took on side jobs as well to create the quality of life he desired. His wife also had a career in which she worked days, nights, weekends, and sometimes holidays. They were willing to put out the extra effort because they had dreams, goals, and wishes.

At work, he was constantly put down; rude remarks and crazy assumptions were thrown at him no matter what he was doing. I coached him, so he could see the real truth behind the unfavorable actions of his coworkers: they were jealous of what he had and who he was striving to be. His success threatened them, so they made every attempt to knock him down to their level. His first thought was of course to react in the same manner, but I helped him realize that would only give them more control, and the best course of action would be to ignore them. They would never be able to see what went on behind the scenes, that what he had, he and his wife had earned—no one handed it to them. Jealousy is a prominent trait of naysayers.

Confidence makes us successful, success does not make us confident.

Your true self-worth is determined by how you value others as well as yourself. You know things about yourself that no one else does. Being honest with yourself comes with wisdom and accepting your imperfections. The more you know yourself, the more freedom you will have because you will learn how to recognize the fears creeping in and how to deal with them. Resist conforming to the image others have of you. Be willing to dream and believe beyond their beliefs.

Add the Bling action step: Ask yourself, "Do I have any evidence or facts that prove I can't accomplish this? If others can do it, why can't I?"

Bling is ignoring pessimists, rising above them, and trusting your own instincts and abilities.

Blah is gossiping and wallowing in others' suffering, defeat and pain.

Never Assume

"You are only limited by your thoughts."

You cannot read minds. Never assume you know what others are thinking, as this will create many wrong assumptions. Everyone has their own agenda, and their actions have nothing to do with you. They are simply fulfilling their wants and needs. When you think you can read others' minds, you get the wrong messages—for example, if someone hasn't returned your email, text, or call in the timeframe you think they should, you conjure up feelings of rejection in your head. Most of the time, the truth is they are just busy with something that is of importance to them and they mean nothing by it, but you assume they are upset with you. Feelings of insecurity, doubt, and fear take over when you think you know what others are thinking. Step back, realize that it really isn't at all as it seems, and instead picture them as being very busy. Maybe something has happened that you don't even know about and that is the reason why they have responded the way they have.

When you make assumptions, situations quickly spiral out of control in the wrong directions. If you leave a message for a friend inviting them to your party and they never respond, all kinds of thoughts start roaming around your head—Are they mad at me? Did I do something wrong?—on and on until you have ruined your own party with your assumptions. A few days later they call to tell you they were sorry they missed your party but their mother was in the hospital. Or someone puts a negative comment on social media that you feel sure was directed at you, and you respond in kind, firing back a less-than-nice response...only to find out it wasn't meant for you, but the next rude comment sure is.

Blah to Bling example: I heard a story about a gentleman who was on the bus. There were several kids running up and down the aisle, yelling, screaming, stepping on others' toes. Their father was just sitting there, not saying a word or trying to control them. The atmosphere was getting tense and tempers were starting to build, so the gentleman decided he would address the situation. He got up and went over to the father. "Sir," he said, "your children are upsetting everyone. Don't you think you should try to calm them down?"

The father looked up at him and said, "I know, I'm sorry." As tears came to his eyes, he explained they had just come from the hospital and their mother had just died. He said, "I don't think they know how to handle it, and quite frankly, I don't either."

The gentleman's mouth flew open. He patted the father on the back and began quietly moving about the car, telling others what was going on. They immediately started to help with the kids, talking to them and getting their minds off the situation. They now gave this man, who a moment ago they were so furious at, a gentle smile and warm welcome. This is a true example of being Exceptional and adding Bling to the world.

An open mind starts with communication with yourself.

You see, if you can just always assume the best instead of the worst, your whole world will change. Remember that when you view the outside world as out to get you, unfriendly, or rude, you really don't have the whole story.

Add the Bling action step: Remind yourself everything isn't always about you, and don't read more into the situation than is necessary.

Bling is not letting others' agendas affect yours. Never assume. Seek the truth and it will set you free.

Blah is allowing yourself to get upset based on assumptions.

Never Compare Yourself to Others

"The only competition is with yourself, to be better than you were yesterday."

There is only one you and you can only ever be yourself, no one else. We are all different, with different strengths and weaknesses. Confidence is acknowledging your weaknesses, committing to improvement, and moving on. You have gifts, strengths, and talents that make you special. Instead of comparing yourself to others, embrace your differences. There is no contest to be yourself; it is only a journey to becoming the best version of yourself. Comparing yourself to others is demeaning: you are judging yourself based on what others can do, which has absolutely nothing to do with you. They have their talents and you have yours, and that is not failure—it only means you vary. Just be you and know that is enough. Believing in yourself is where confidence begins. Believe all things are possible and they will be yours.

You compare yourself to others when there is a big party so you buy a new outfit, get all dressed up and feel like a million bucks, but when you arrive you spot several others who look nice and you start allowing negative thoughts about how you look compared to them ruin your night.

Or you buy a wedding gift for a friend, carefully selected based on their likes, however when they start opening more expensive gifts, you begin to feel like yours isn't as good as the others. Your thought is the most valuable gift.

Or you enter a 5k race, which you have never done before, and place 3rd. Although having the courage to try something new and placing at all in your first attempt is winning, you soon put yourself down because you didn't take first.

Blah to Bling example: In my job as a realtor, my broker would have contests in which we would compete against one another. At meetings, those who had the highest dollar amount in sales would get all the recognition while others would sit in the shadows and get no credit for their efforts. This was very demoralizing to those who didn't meet the standards of the contests—many of them had worked just as hard, closed just as many or more transactions, and in reality, had been very successful, but their successes were compared to the success of others. This caused many to wonder "What's the point?" and give up. The best way to motivate yourself and others is to encourage results be measured against your own previous results, only striving to be better today than you were yesterday. If you made another sale, or even made an extra effort toward more sales, you are a true winner.

We are all capable of great success. Others' achievements have nothing to do with our accomplishments.

The most important thing to remember is there is no contest to be you. Never fret about the successes of others. Simply put your best effort forward in all you do; there are many rewards for being your best self and none of them can ever be taken away from you by others' accomplishments. The only way you do not win is if you settle for less than your best.

Add the Bling action step: When the urge arises to compare your results to someone else's, remind yourself the only comparison is against your own results. You can only be your best self and nothing else matters.

Bling is comparing your results today with your results from yesterday to improve yourself.

Blah is comparing yourself to others, competing to be better than them.

Your Beliefs Write Your Life's Story

"Without realizing who you are, you cannot find happiness."

Emotions control your thoughts, but most of the time they have no basis in truth. Negative emotions trigger thoughts that will lead you down the wrong path. Examine your thoughts, constantly looking for substantiated facts to back the belief being created by your thoughts. Your beliefs began with thoughts, so if you don't keep a close watch on your thoughts, you will soon have many beliefs that have absolutely no truth behind them. Refuse thoughts that you are not good enough or smart enough to accomplish something you are dreaming of, because before you know it, you start to accept them as truth.

Most of the information you hear is nothing more than the beliefs of others. You should listen with an open mind because you cannot learn and grow if you do not remain open to other perspectives. However, you must only allow something to become a belief of yours if it meets your values, goals, and dreams. Always ask yourself when something is suggested, "Is this really true or is it simply what they believe to be true?" Others are not trying to lead you astray with their beliefs; they simply have accepted what has been told to them and it has become true to them because that is all they know. You can only accomplish what you believe in, so don't let others sway you with their beliefs.

Always follow your moral compass: when you know in your heart what is right but choose to ignore it, you feel incomplete. You sell yourself short. It takes courage to do what is right and good, but if you follow your conscience and develop your beliefs, you will find freedom.

Following your own beliefs is when you walk away from discussions you don't agree with. Imagine you like your job and enjoy working there, but in the break room others are discussing how it is a terrible place to work, the pay is bad, and the schedule is unfair. Others soon chime in and now they are all convinced it is a terrible place to work, so you excuse yourself from the room because you do not share their beliefs. Or you feel great when you arrive at a party, however everyone is discussing the latest disease they've heard about, and before you know it, everyone seems to have a symptom and isn't feeling well. You yourself begin to think you feel a bit dizzy, maybe a little flushed. Thoughts begin to fill your mind: "I am getting sick?" Are you? or was that belief planted there?

Blah to Bling example: If a sports announcer said, "This team is going to lose this game; they will never win. Sure, they have talented people and a good strategy, but they will never win. It isn't possible; I am telling you they will fail," would you follow that team? Would you watch that game? That's what is wrong with the health industry:

they give us a death sentence, telling us it is terminal—you will have sickness and disease because it is in your genes, you have cancer, get things in order, you are going to die.

No kidding, we are all going to die someday, but when we accept their lies, we surely are going to die sooner. If they would give hope and courage, guidance, tools, and education on avoidance instead of the vision of gloom, we could cure most illnesses. Worst case scenario is we enjoy our last days hoping and believing we have a chance instead of resolving to die and giving up. If we give up hope, we are surely dead even if we are still breathing. Most people think false hope is cruel or wrong—really? Life without hope is cruel and deadlier than cancer. The crime isn't in believing, it is in taking away others' power to believe.

Our greatest source of beliefs is what we say to ourselves

Until you get to the root of a weed and destroy it, it will continue to grow back faster and bigger each time, becoming stronger and more resilient. Your thoughts and beliefs are the same way: the more you allow them to flourish, the stronger they get, so you must constantly strive for your own beliefs. Until you gain belief you will never have control of anything in your life.

Add the Bling action step: Keep a watchful eye out for outside forces that mold your beliefs: your social life, media, movies, others' thoughts and beliefs. Outside thoughts are the troublemakers for inside thoughts.

Bling is choosing your own beliefs and not allowing others' beliefs to become yours.

Blah is allowing ourselves to believe others without thinking for ourselves.

I Am Responsible

"They say that time changes things, but you actually have to change them yourself."

Responsibility means empowerment; it doesn't mean you are to blame as you sometimes think, or that you have done something wrong and must be punished or feel shame. It means you are taking charge and you can change your circumstances or situation at will.

You are not responsible for other people's actions; they are, and they must take ownership of their actions, not you. What you are, however, responsible for is how you act in response to their actions. When you react, you behave in response to the actions of others; to act means to take action. When your actions are based on your values and beliefs instead of someone else's, that is responsibility.

For instance, if you value honesty but telling the truth about something will create issues with others who wish to twist the truth to suit them, when you refuse to give up your values no matter the consequences, you have taken responsibility. If you believe in something that others are demeaning and you keep quiet and go along, your actions are not in line with your beliefs. This is not always easy because when someone does something you do not approve of, it can ignite anger, fear, jealousy, and many other feelings which will steal your control.

The day you take complete responsibility for yourself, the day you stop making excuses, that's the day you start your journey to the top.

You can start right now, in this very minute, to take responsibility, to change your direction and to actually decide your destiny. You can launch the Take Back Your Life Plan anytime you wish; it all starts with you deciding you are responsible and nobody else. I know what you are thinking—"But you don't understand! Your life isn't like mine. You don't have the health problems, husband, job..." (Fill in the blank with whatever your excuse is, because that is all it is—an excuse.) Making excuses means you have not taken responsibility for your choices and actions. There are circumstances, tragedies, and life events that happen and will continue to happen that you have no control over, that is true, but it is how you choose to act in response to them that decides your destiny.

You can allow the power thieves—anger, jealousy, greed, self-pity—to steal your thunder, or you can be the lightning that strikes with precision and accuracy. When you realize that you are responsible for every one of your actions (I know what thought just flashed through your mind: "I may be responsible for most things, but not everything!"), you are in control. This can be very hard to wrap your mind around; I know it was for me. You are thinking, "How can this abusive husband, health issue, (again, fill in the blank, because everyone has a different blank to fill in) be my fault?" Stop, take a step back, and understand that you cannot control life, but you can control your actions in response to the curves, potholes, and bumps life throws at you.

Blah to Bling example: Things become your fault based on your choices. Maybe you are texting, putting on your makeup, and driving all at the same time because you are very busy and have a thousand things you have to do before you get to work, when—wham! —you collide with the car beside of you. They crossed over into your lane. What were they thinking? Did they hit you, or did you hit them? Could it have been avoided if you were watching the road?

That is your fault! It was your choices that led up to this accident. No, you didn't mean to get hit (that's why they call it an accident), but you are responsible for your actions. You chose to allow yourself to be distracted; you gave up your power. If you had been paying attention, you maybe could have avoided the collision. No one can take your power from you unless you allow them.

I realize at this point you may not believe this or want to accept this simple fact, but the sooner you do, the sooner you will move forward. As hard as it may seem, when you can look in the mirror and say, "I AM RESPONSIBLE," your life will change. When you end the blame game, you can get down to the business of empowering your life. You can't fix something that you haven't accepted is broken; you have to accept that you are responsible for your actions and results, because until you take ownership, you cannot fix the problem.

When you take responsibility for your actions, your eyes will be opened to a whole new world of opportunities. You will no longer have to live with guilt, regrets, and lies or make excuses for missed opportunities. No more grudges, hard feelings, or needless arguments because you will quit blaming others for circumstances. You will begin to see the world in a totally different light—you will see that you really gain power by giving up your false beliefs that everything is someone else's fault. When you face this objective reality, the cloud of delusion will be lifted from your life.

All is earned, not given, and life is what you make it, not circumstances.

You do not control all life hands you, but facing it as your responsibility and no one else's gives you the control to decide how to handle it. You are only entitled to what you get by way of effort, creating your own worth, building your character, using your mind to create. You cannot sit idle and expect things to be handed to you; the only thing you are entitled to is your right to think, make choices, and create your destiny. Taking responsibility for yourself and your actions sets you free from the victim mentality and puts you in the position to *act* instead of *react.*

At the end of the day, we are accountable to ourselves—our success is a result of what we do.

If your life has gone in the wrong direction—drugs, alcohol, failed relationships, or whatever it may be—

don't blame it on a poor upbringing. By taking responsibility for your actions, you have the power to turn things around. Accept that just because others made bad choices does not give you the excuse to do the same.

Taking responsibility is setting your own alarm, getting up on time and arriving at work on early. It's not blaming someone for getting you up late or screaming at the slow driver in front of you making you late. You created the circumstances surrounding you. Accepting this gives you the power of control.

Being responsible is not blaming fast food restaurants for your health or weight issues. Yes, they may offer highly addictive, high-calorie foods and push the super-size option on you. But you have the responsibility to not go there. They do not force you to eat it; you choose to.

Your life choices are all your fault. The blame is on you. Reminding yourself of this fact is how you become responsible.

Add the Bling action step: When things don't go as planned, don't whine, complain, or blame—take responsibility and change it.

Bling is taking responsibility even when you feel it isn't your fault.

Blah is blaming others for your circumstances.

Forgive and Let Live

"Forgiveness is not just about the other. It's for the beauty of your soul."

L ive is meant to be lived. It is about creating memories and not living with regrets. You are not perfect; life happens, circumstances are sometimes beyond your control, and at times you feel like you have been dealt a bad hand. Confidence is moving beyond that, accepting that it is what it is, and working toward creating new memories that will cause the old ones to fade away. Living a life of regret is like living a bad dream over and over. Wake up and make your dreams what you desire; don't allow the past to darken your future.

Don't let yesterday use up too much of today.

Holding on to grudges holds you down. When you are angry at others, they have control over you because your thoughts are being held captive, which affects your actions, attitude, and results. By allowing your thoughts to dwell on what is bothering you, you have given the other party control, and most times, truth be known, they have moved on and forgotten all about it. The best way to win that battle is to forgive them and forget it. Forgiving and forgetting releases all the anger, pain, and resentment trapped inside of you.

Forgiving is when someone you love decides that the relationship you are in isn't working, and you accept their wishes, although you are hurt. You realize if they are not happy, it is for the better that you no longer be together, and you wish them well without holding on to anger.

You can show forgiveness when someone is late, and they never called to let you know they would be extremely late. You can ruin the rest of the day fuming over how they kept you waiting, how inconsiderate they are, or you can forget about it and make the most of the time you now have together.

Or maybe you promised yourself you would eat better but you slip up and find yourself on the couch with a bag of chips. Put them down, forget about it, and vow to eat a healthy dinner. Forgiving your weakness is the first step to improvement.

Sometimes the person you need to forgive most is yourself. You beat yourself up over mistakes you have made, things you have said or not said. You cannot change the past—however, you can create the future. Learn from the past, but don't let it hold you prisoner.

Blah to Bling example: Richard was completely blindsided when his wife told him she no longer wanted to be married. She said she still loved him, but the situation wasn't working for her. As the years went by after the divorce, there were many heartaches. Her guilt kept her from visiting her daughter, which caused hurt feelings. He couldn't let it go, always hanging on and allowing the past to destroy his present. Hurt, anger, and much resentment ruled his life. I urged him to let it go before it destroyed him, but he allowed his emotions to continue to control his life, dwelling on the wrong she had done to him and, even more devastating, how she had hurt their daughter.

She moved on, got remarried, and now tries to be a part of her daughter's life. Although the daughter had been hurt by her actions, she decided it was better for her to forgive and forget. This small decision put her in control again while her father still struggles. He makes many bad decisions because he bases his choices on his emotions instead of on his clear thinking.

When we make choices based on emotions, we constantly question our decisions, feeling that they were wrong because others may not have accepted them. By dwelling on thoughts of what he could have done differently so she would not have left, he gives up his power. Instead, he needs to forgive himself (mostly because there was no fault on his part anyway), because it's the only way to forgive her and then forget all the bad memories, keep the good ones, and learn from the experience.

Add the Bling action step: Forgive others for their mistakes and trespasses against you or others and forget it ever happened. Forgiving is only the first step; forgetting is the Exceptional step.

Bling is dropping the baggage of the past, forgiving yourself and others, and moving onward and upward.

Blah is holding on to hurt feelings, regrets, and bottled up anger, giving up your power.

I Am Willing to Pay the Price

"Pain is inevitable. Suffering is optional."

Everything has a price: victory cannot be won without the battle; one cannot be had without the other. You must be willing to pay to achieve your goals, and although you wish you could find the sale of a lifetime, understand that you get what you pay for. Do not get upset or discouraged at obstacles; simply face them head on with courage. Accepting the price that must be paid to have what you want and being willing to pay it makes you stronger. Always remember why you are doing it and pay full price—you don't want to discount your future.

Paying the price is staying home to study for an exam when your friends invite you out for drinks, so you can do well in the night classes you are taking to get a better job. Or skipping the pizza you want for lunch because you are going on vacation in a month and want to look better in your swimsuit. Or giving up eating out, your Starbucks, or buying extra luxuries because you are saving to buy a car so you don't have to deal with the bus anymore.

Blah To Bling

The path to success begins with the pain of change but evolves into euphoria as feelings of fulfillment arise. Fight the fight—it is well worth it. When fatigue, frustration, and impatience creep in, stay focused. The only easy way out is to give in and accept average, and that is no way to live. Don't be afraid—what is the worst that can happen? Life cannot be survived. In the end, we all must die. However, you do have the choice to live every day you are given, making the most of it and of yourself. Safe and comfortable is boring.

Blah to Bling example: George had a job with the phone company that paid a good wage with benefits. He did very well and made all his sales quotas and received bonuses. The position was in a call center in which you were literally strapped to the phone all day. There were many demands, restrictions, and rules and often some very unpleasant customers.

He had taken the job with the promise of moving into a sales consultant position where he would help others improve their skills, which would allow him to travel to other offices. Sadly, there was a freeze put on transfers not long after he got the job, and he was forced to remain in the call center.

He hated his job. On his way home Friday, he would begin to dread going to work on Monday. His worries and regrets began to overtake his peace of mind. He wanted to quit, but constantly heard how lucky he was to have such a good job— "If you just stick it out 30 years, you will be set!"

His health began to suffer: he was stressed, depressed, and very unhappy. He decided that staying there was the equivalent of a prison sentence, and he was not willing to give up 30 years of his life. He walked away from that job. Leaving that building was a very freeing moment for him.

He certainly faced many struggles afterward finding a career to pay the bills; he had to change his lifestyle, sell some things, and work very hard. There were quite a few lean years before he built a new career; he went through many failures and mistakes trying to start other businesses that flopped. But he never gave up. Even when things looked dim and they offered him his old job back, he kept moving toward his dreams, no matter what price he had to pay.

Blah to Bling action step: When faced with a decision, first take time to write down at least three things you will gain and three or more struggles you will have to endure. Carefully make your decision based on what your true desires are and understand the sacrifices for achieving them.

Bling is deciding to push through the pain to receive what you truly desire.

Blah is deluding yourself into thinking there will be no pain on the road to your success.

Create your own luck

"The harder you work the luckier you will be"

W hat you accomplish is through perseverance, hard work, and dedication. Life isn't just for the lucky few; it is for all who know that they are a direct outcome of their efforts, that the playing field is equal. Waiting for the lucky break that never seems to come sucks the confidence right out of you because it is a game of chance. You create your own luck. Go after it, don't sit on the porch waiting on it.

Creating your own luck is setting out to learn the skills you need to start your own business instead of thinking, "I can't be successful like others because I don't have their luck." Or asking out that special guy instead of using the excuse "I'm not lucky enough to be as smart or pretty as the other girls." Or entering the contest even though the odds are overwhelming instead of convincing yourself there's no point because you're "not lucky" anyway.

Luck is found when we dare to see beyond what our eyes see and take a chance.

You cannot change the seasons, circumstances, or the wind, but you can change yourself. No one and nothing is coming to rescue you; all you are and ever will be is up to you, so don't place any bets on anything else. All your decisions, indecisions, actions, and lack of action have added up to create the life you are living—luck or no luck had nothing to do with it. Remember, there are takers who hope that life will be good to them, that they get lucky, and there are makers who get the most out of life by giving the best they have and being the best they can be.

Blah to Bling example: Christopher was viewed as the luckiest guy in town, he had a beautiful home, drove an expensive car, prestigious career, charming, loving wife and family, lots of friends, was in good health and everything just seemed to go his way. Everyone would grumble about how it "must be nice to be lucky" or how "it's just not fair that some people have it all"

What they didn't see was the long hours Christopher worked, many days of travel away from home for business. The way he cared for his family and friends, taking time for them and going the extra mile to be kind, caring and compassionate even when he was tired or maybe didn't feel like it. The days off he spent manicuring the lawn or maintaining his home, so it looked nice. They weren't there when his alarm went off at 5 am so he could work out and prepare a healthy lunch, so he could be healthy.

All they could see was his results that they presumed was all because he was lucky. What they didn't realize was his luck was met with hard work and consistent effort.

Add the Bling action step: Resist saying, "I am just not lucky." Instead, get out there and create your luck. Tell yourself every day, "I am so lucky," and you soon will be.

Bling is creating your own luck, not counting on the lottery of life to bring to you what you desire. It's going out and making it happen yourself.

Blah is being lazy, settling for current circumstances because you just aren't lucky.

This Too Shall Pass

"Prepare to go the distance; quitting is not an option."

Nothing lasts forever, and everything happens for a reason, so don't wallow in fear, worry, and doubt. This will poison your thoughts and derail your progress. Push through to the other side knowing no pain, struggle, defeat, or failure can stop you. The key is to not allow the event to continue. Identify its cause and work to correct it to avoid the setback in the future. If your expectation is that a well-run life should always be orderly, you are setting yourself up for panic and defeat. Things will work out, but maybe not just as you planned, so accept it and be grateful it isn't worse. Viewing the world with this perspective will give you total power and control over your life. Knowing that no matter how bad the situation may seem, it could be even worse makes dealing with what faces you a little easier to handle.

Embrace the suck to achieve the dream.

A good example of reminding yourself that something will pass is an illness. Although it may be causing total havoc in your life, reminding yourself that you will soon be better, and your life will get back on track (even if it is a new track) will help you push through.

Another example is when your work schedule is crazy, stressful, and demanding due to a special project or holiday season. When this happens, focus on the thought that it isn't forever. Or maybe you went back to school to improve your future and you are stressed with a full schedule of work and school. Envision the future benefits, remind yourself it is only a temporary thing, and the pain will be less.

Keeping your focus on the circumstance, result, or event beyond the current situation is the key to getting past the current event causing discomfort.

Blah to Bling example: One of the strongest, bravest ladies I have ever known is Jan Bernard. She always gave her best in all she did, no matter what she was facing.

Jan worked full-time as a realtor. She was known as the "first lady of real estate," and taught real estate school two nights a week and Saturdays. She was big participant in her church, belonged to many organizations, donated her time, and was very dedicated to her family. When Jan was diagnosed with cancer, she never let it keep her down—she went to treatments and then off to her work right after. She spent many years struggling with low blood counts, emergency visits to the hospital, and far more than any of us can imagine. Through it all she still kept her commitments. Even when she didn't feel well and should have stayed home, she did not; she never let her circumstances keep her down. She always kept the faith that this too shall pass.

Although the world lost Jan, up till her last days, she had a positive attitude. Jan will forever be an inspiration to me. On my last visit with her, which was only days before her passing, she was encouraging me and asking about my life without a thought to her situation. When I want to stay in bed, feel sorry for myself, worry about my situation, or consider giving up, I think to myself, "Jan never gave up. Why should you?" In loving memory of Jan, never give up, always be your best, and you will have nothing to fear.

Add the Bling action step: Imagine the worst-case scenario, remind yourself nothing is forever, and be grateful for what you do have.

Bling is remembering, when you think all is lost, that the future remains, and it's the hard times that make you Exceptional.

Blah is giving up when things get tough and accepting ordinary because Exceptional is just too hard.

Choose to Be a Warrior, Not a Worrier

"Power versus force is the key to a winning outcome."

D o not sit on the sidelines of your life filled with worry, doubt, and fear. Don't let the what ifs control you; instead say, "Why not me?", put it all on the line, and go for it. You cannot win the battle if you are not even in it, so you must step beyond your worries. Be the warrior of your life, willing to fight to achieve something greater than your fears, something in the unknown beyond your comfort zone, something beyond where you are now and who you are now.

Doubt is the cause of worry.

Doubt is merely the lack of faith; it derails you. When you doubt yourself, your abilities, or someone else, you are setting in motion a controlling force. If you set out to accomplish something and, in your mind you doubt it will ever happen, you have set your course. Your thoughts and beliefs guide you through life, even when you don't realize it. Have you ever done something and after the fact said to yourself, "Why did I do that?" You didn't even realize you did it and have no clue why, but it's because your thoughts simply led you to that.

Doubt is a thought, nothing more. It is not the same as fear. When you fear something, you avoid it if possible because fear is an emotion of discomfort. Doubt, on the other hand, is a perception you have of something, someone, or yourself. All things are possible to those who believe, yet most of the time we do not. The purpose of this book is to help you gain confidence. However deeply embedded in your mind your doubt that will ever happen is, you must put aside your doubting self. You say, "I want to change, I want to become confident and successful," and without even realizing it, the wheels of doubt are spinning out of control. Although you want to make a change, your thoughts of doubt control your destiny. You can only become what you believe in; your hopes and dreams will not come to you until you believe.

Once you start to doubt yourself, worry is almost automatic. Did you ever have plans outside that needed nice weather, such as a picnic or a wedding? Before you knew it, your mind started to conjure up all sorts of worries: it is going to rain, everything will be ruined. Next thing you know, your worries were running rampant, coming up with scenarios that were never going to happen—but in your mind, they were real. So real that sometimes you just forgot all about even doing it and thought about just staying home. You give up on your dreams because of your worries, which result from doubt.

Many of the things keeping you from becoming confident are directly related to one another, as you can see. They are all part of a huge trap, and unless you become aware of them, you can't take the steps to overcome each one.

Doubt is a killer. You just have to know who you are and what you stand for.

Doubt can only be overcome by replacing it with belief; you can never truly eliminate it. It will always be lurking around, ready to spring into action when you least need it. You must recognize this feeling will come up—no one lives without doubt or fear, they merely learn to control it. We give it to others all the time and others give it to us without even realizing it. You may have your mind made up, truly believe you can accomplish something, and then someone plants the tiny seed of doubt in you and it grows out of control, choking the roots of your belief.

Why do you allow others to steal your dreams and ambitions? It's because the seed of doubt is always inside of you and if you let others fertilize it with words of fear, disbelief, and worry, it will always grow. You ask yourself, "Why do others want to do this to me?" but the truth is that most of the time, they don't intentionally destroy your beliefs, they live in doubt themselves. The things you fear come out in the form of doubt. You don't even see or hear it, but there it is, out in the open for all to see.

A good example of doubt: you decide you want to move to a new area where there is more opportunity. You have done your homework, checked out jobs, housing, and the area, and you are very excited. Then someone says, "Why would you want to move there?" and the flood of doubt and fear begins. What if I can't find a job, what if things don't work out—before you know it, the what ifs have taken over and you talk yourself right out of it.

Keep in mind, things may not work out where you are now. There are no guarantees in life, so don't let your doubts and fears keep you from getting out there and giving life a chance.

You are strong. Fear will not defeat you.

You can never control the doubts of others, but you can manage your own: when you keep your beliefs strong, you can keep doubts at bay. Once you have built a strong barrier around your beliefs, it is much harder for others' doubts to penetrate your thoughts.

Blah to Bling example: I myself had always been a worrier; I worried about everything, which stressed me out. I couldn't even live in the moment because of all my worries about tomorrow. The what ifs kept me stuck in the same place, kept me from my confidence, until I realized and accepted they were only thoughts in my mind, nothing more. They had to be pushed aside with feelings of security, which come through our beliefs. I developed mantras that I would repeat over and over when my internal worries attempted to derail me or create doubt. Two of my favorites are, "I can do anything I want if I just keep believing I can," and "What will be will be, this too shall pass." You are strong. Fear will not defeat you and worry brings you no victories; only fighting the battle brings you closer to your desires and passions.

Add the Bling action step: When you catch yourself worrying, remind yourself that most of what you worry about will never be and all the worry in the world will not solve the issue. Worry is procrastination in disguise.

Bling is going to battle with your worries and fears and never letting them keep you from your dreams.

Blah is allowing your worries to keep you from your best self.

All I Really Have Is Now

"Don't live in the past or always be dreaming of tomorrow. Act like the person you want to be now."

Serenity is found when you are fully aware of the moment. There are two days a week you can forget because they are not important: yesterday and tomorrow. Life is better, and confidence is found when you enjoy the perfect moment of now. Learn to love yourself as you are today because you cannot bring better results until you do.

Here's a perfect example: you want to lose weight, so you make it your New Year's resolution. You put off everything until you do, telling yourself you will be happy once you lose weight. You are so busy living in the future world, you miss all the beautiful moments of today like a piece of birthday cake at someone special's party, or you skip an important event because you don't think you look good enough yet.

Or you find yourself in a very common situation: you work night and day, so you can buy something, telling yourself it will make your life so much better. You miss time with family and friends, and you are tired all the time, so even when you are around others, you are not much fun. You eat on the run, settling for whatever is quick and easy. When you finally get what you were working for (that is, if you ever get it), you are too tired and stressed to appreciate it anyway.

Happiness is found in the precious moments of today, not in the hopes of tomorrow.

You will make mistakes, but that's OK. Don't waste your precious energy holding on to what you should be letting go of. Stop trying to change things that you cannot change; it keeps you from enjoying the present moment. Always focus on the present while planning for the future. Being fully present, fully engaged with others, makes a huge impact. Genuine focus and attention makes you mesmerizing.

Blah to Bling example: Sally had a good life with a loving family and friends, a good job, a nice home, and so much more, however she didn't seem to realize this. She was always busy worrying about how she should have gone to college, so she could be making more money and fretting over how she should have started saving for retirement sooner, should have exercised more, should have eaten better. She was should-ing herself to death. Her thoughts were consumed with having enough money for retirement, her health in her later years, and on and on.

Her days were filled with such worries of yesterday and tomorrow that she often skipped events, put off doing things, and didn't even hear the conversations going on around her because her head was so full of worries—until one day, her doctor gave her some disturbing news. He had found a tumor and surgery along with treatment would be needed to hopefully save her life.

In an instant, nothing in the past mattered any longer and there might not be a future. For the first time in her life, she opened her eyes and saw all the wonderful things she had in her life. She started cherishing every moment with her family, enjoying every sunset, never missing an event or special occasion. She cared for herself very carefully, taking time to plan healthy meals and getting some activity and plenty of rest. All of these things were right in front of her all of her life, but she hadn't seen them for the clouds of yesterday and storms of tomorrow. The good news is that Sally is once again well, and she lives a healthy, mindful life. Don't wait for lightning to strike you to see what is in front of you now.

Add the Bling action step: Write down the traits and qualities you desire and then act like the person you wish to become today. The more you play the role, the quicker you will achieve the results you desire while still appreciating today.

Bling is accepting who you are now, living your life today, and enjoying the joy of the moment.

Blah is living in the past or the future and missing out on today.

Always Be Prepared

"Not having a plan is a plan to fail."

Being prepared is what earns you confidence—it isn't just given, it is earned. Put in the work to prepare for anything you are doing, and you will be amazed by how confident you will be. Tackle your goals with the knowledge that you are prepared—this removes doubt and fear. Practice is another form of preparing. It makes you better, and the better you become, the more confident you become. Opportunity finds you when you prepare, and it passes you by when you don't: you will get what you deserve. Good ideas, creativity, and good fortune come to you when you seek to become better, learn, and grow.

Being prepared is having your resumé ready, selecting a nice outfit in advance, and arriving early instead of throwing it together the night before, realizing the morning of the interview you have nothing suitable to wear, and waiting till the last minute to leave, not allowing for traffic.

Being prepared means picking up all the ingredients for cupcakes for your daughter's bake sale in advance, so you don't have to stop at the store on the way home from work when you are running late. Not being prepared means running in and grabbing day-old cupcakes at the bakery because you don't have time to bake.

Being prepared means taking time to order a very special gift for your mom that you know she really wants instead of settling for a gift card because you waited until the last minute.

The Exceptional prepare and review every detail in advance—that is where they get their confidence.

Life is full of obstacles, challenges, and hurdles, but confidence is what keeps them from becoming roadblocks or tragedies. Preparedness is what keeps you from possible defeat, not luck or chance. There will always be things flung at you to knock you off your game. Having a plan is how you overcome and rise above instead of settling for what happens.

Blah to Bling example: Sally wanted to be a trainer within her company, and there was a good position opening up the following year when one of her colleagues was retiring. The problem was, she was scared to death of getting up in front of anyone, let alone a room full of her peers.

She asked her friend how she had the courage to do it, how she could be so confident in front of the room. She said, "I could never do that! I wish I was born with your talents."

Her friend laughed hysterically and said, "I was scared out of my mind at first, but I prepared, practiced, and prepared some more." She explained that although she had now been doing this for 30 years, she still always over-prepared for every session because that is what gave her courage and confidence. She explained that by always having a plan, she could always handle any issues that might arise. She lived by the premise that you can never be too prepared. She encouraged Sally to start practicing and preparing for the position because talents, skills, and confidence develop over time, and no one is born with them, no matter how in control they may appear.

Add the Bling action step: Never assume you know it all or that you do not need to prepare to be your best. Always have a plan and a back-up plan; prepare for the worst and you will be amazed at how great it all turns out.

Bling is constantly practicing, planning, and striving to be better, no matter how good you think you are. Perfect is the death of success, because it doesn't exist.

Blah is assuming you are good enough without preparation and allowing yourself to settle for OK.

The Past Does Not Determine the Future

"The past does not determine the future unless we allow it."

Memories can be tricky. When you recall an event or circumstance, you sometimes remember how you felt more than the event itself, which can cloud your perception of how it really was. You may have felt worried, doubtful, or hurt, so when you recall the event, those feeling take over and guide what you remember. Many times, you have a distorted memory of events and what really happened is nothing like what you remember. That can lead to letting memories keep you from doing what you really want.

Do you tell yourself you can't do something because you were terrible at it as a child and you have a painful childhood memory, so you don't even try to do it now? Maybe you were in a school play and you panicked, forgot your lines, and ran off stage, so now the thought of getting up in front of a group causes feelings of fear and embarrassment because you "think" you are not good at it. So you avoid it even though becoming a trainer at work would be a huge advancement.

Or maybe as a teenager you were scrawny and sickly and you remember being told you will always have to deal with illness, you will always be smaller than everyone else. So when you are admiring strong, stout people, you don't even try to adopt their habits to build your strength and immunity because you have allowed your memories to convince you that it isn't possible for you to do that.

Think about what you want, and forget the past. You are what you think about.

The past is no more. You have no control over it, and it does not define you, deter you, or defeat you. Do not let the past steal the present or the future. Your past is not your identity. It may have helped you become stronger, but don't become a prisoner to it—your power lies in the now.

Blah to Bling example: As child, Roberta had a very vivid imagination. She loved drawing and creating and dreamed of being an artist someday. However, she was constantly told "Don't waste your time. There are many starving artists. Get a real job so you can pay the bills." She eventually quit drawing altogether, went on with her life, and got what others referred to as a "real job."

Many years later, she was doodling and sketched a picture in the notebook she took to meetings for notes when one of her team members spotted it and commented on how good it was. They said, "You should have been an artist."

Roberta quickly replied, "I tried, but I just wasn't good enough, I couldn't pay the bills."

They said, "Really? How long did you try? Maybe you just needed to stick with it a little longer."

In reality, she had never tried to fulfill her dream. She had given up due to others' comments, but when she thought back on it, she remembered it as failing, and that became her memory. There was no truth to it, just a deluded memory.

Add the Bling action step: When your memories of an event upset you, ask yourself, "Is that the way it really happened, or is that just how I remember it?" What happened doesn't matter—all that matters is what you learned from it to make yourself better.

Bling is learning to refocus on the real facts, not a delusional memory that keeps you from moving forward.

Blah is allowing past circumstance to define who you are.

Mistakes Are a Learning Experience

"Success is not final, failure is not fatal. It is the courage to continue that counts."

You will fail and that is OK. Anything worth doing is worth doing badly till you master it. Don't put off doing something you want to do because you think you are not good at it; start doing it now and keep at it until you get good. Successful people don't start out that way; they had to embrace discomfort until they mastered their talents. We view successful people as being born with their talent, but if you were to ask any of them, they would tell you that their talent came from consistent action, practice, and time, it didn't just magically appear.

We all make mistakes. I'm sure, you at some point tried a new recipe that flopped. You didn't quit cooking, you just kept trying new recipes. The first time you attempted to drive a car you didn't get behind the wheel and off you went. No, I'm sure you were corrected by your instructor numerous times and maybe even hit a few things before you figured it out.

Failure is practice, not the finish line.

Get real: preparing for failure is the only way to succeed. Fear of failure will hold you captive. Failure is an inevitable fact of life unless you choose to never try. If someone tells you they have never failed, feel very sorry for them, because they are in denial—or worse yet, never crawled out from under their rock into the real world. Success does not happen in your comfort zone; it grows out in the big scary world of chance. Realize the start of success is a series of failures, and remember that you never truly fail unless you give up. Failure at the moment simply means you didn't get it right this time, but with this knowledge, you can move on to success. Mistakes simply mean we don't know yet!

Blah to Bling example: In the movie *Eddie the Eagle*, a young man wanted to become an Olympic skier. He was awkward and lacked coordination and skills. Although everyone made fun of him and told him he could never do it, he never gave up. He failed over and over again, and he even got seriously hurt many times, yet he never accepted failure. He just kept practicing and learning. He did alter his plan and choose a different division of skiing, but he never gave up on his dream, even when it looked different from his original version. He could have accepted defeat when he failed the first couple of times, but he refused to give in and stayed true to himself. His true fulfillment came from his dedication to trying, not from the final event.

Add the Bling action step: Choose someone you admire for their talents, and ask them how they achieved their success. This will help you understand you too can do the thing you wish to do because you will realize they weren't just born with their skills and you didn't miss your chance.

Watch the movie *Eddie the Eagle*.

Bling is jumping in, getting up when you fall, not getting discouraged, and never giving up.

Blah is never starting because of your fear of failure.

Section 2: Traits

Developing Distinguishing Qualities

A distinguishing quality or characteristic is a trait. It is something you have based on your values and goals. Your traits help to determine your destiny because your traits define who you are. The Exceptional have developed successful, honorable, value-based habits that become traits of their personality, making them who they are.

We all have traits; the key is developing the ones you don't have that will yield the results desired. You may also uncover some traits you have that you may be better off replacing with some of the ones described in this section.

To add Bling to your life, study the traits of the Exceptional and add them to your life!

Confidence

"Confidence creates calm."

Accepting yourself is the first step to confidence—if you are not comfortable with yourself, it will always show. When faced with challenging circumstances, you must respond in the way you want to be viewed, even if there is total chaos inside. Act with self-assurance, never giving a hint of your fears. Being viewed as in control and not frazzled will build upon your confidence and help you maintain your cool in the hottest situations.

Confidence determines ability.

When you have great ideas and want to share them with others, you must first believe in yourself. If you are trying to sell an idea, you can't present it with a wishy-washy attitude; you must deliver it with conviction and enthusiasm. If others sense doubt in you, they will not take your ideas seriously. Being self-assured doesn't mean they will always accept your ideas, but it does give you the edge. Deliver your ideas with complete confidence: believe they are good ideas that deserve consideration, that they will add value to others or the situation. If questioned, don't automatically assume they are right and you are wrong. Don't give up on your ideas so easily.

Having confidence is discovering your truest best friend within. Imagine having someone you truly believe in, someone you know you can count no matter what. Someone you are comfortable with no matter how you look, if you're having the worst day of your life, or if you've just made the biggest mistake. They are there, accepting and encouraging you with unconditional love. Self-love needs to be constant and limitless always.

Of course, you want to have that feeling because without it you have negative, self-defeating voices controlling you. When you tell yourself you are fat, ugly, or stupid or don't believe you can do something, it destroys you from the inside out. You wouldn't talk to your best friend like that; they would get mad and throw you out of their life (I hope!). So why do you tolerate it from yourself?

Lack of confidence is all around us, although all you may see is confident, successful people, making you feel like you are all alone. The most confident people on the outside are fighting the fight against despair daily as well. The difference is they refuse to let it take over, so they work at building and securing their confidence daily. This is not a possession available for a few; it is there for the taking of all who decide to fight for what is rightfully theirs.

Confidence appears when you prepare yourself. For instance: you have a sales presentation, so you get all the facts, benefits, and possible objections together. When you are questioned you can answer with total confidence because you took time to prepare. If you play sports, you practice over and over until you can perform with confidence. Confidence is nothing more than practice and preparedness.

Everything in your life is affected by your confidence: health, income, relationships, happiness, security. By gaining your self-confidence, you can change your life. Maybe you had it at some point and lost it—that is easily done if you don't keep an eye on it. It is a very slippery slope and once you allow yourself to slide, self-doubt becomes an avalanche that buries your self-esteem and you lose yourself. You then become who others force you to be and that is usually not anything you wish to be.

Blah to Bling example: Misty has dreams trapped inside of her: to build a business, to land that great position, to lose weight, to find that special someone, to look in the mirror and like the image staring back at her, to become friends with that voice within. But none of those things seem possible.

The door slams and jars her from her negative stupor, and in walks little Miss Confident. She has everything Misty desires. She sits down beside her and offers her some of her healthy lunch—"Of course she is eating a salad while I eat pizza," thinks Misty. Miss Confident asks her what her plans are for the weekend, and Misty replies, "I don't know yet," even though she knows she won't do anything exciting.

Miss Confident tells Misty that she is attending a conference in which she hopes to learn some skills to start a new career, and she invites Misty to go with her. Before she can reply, Miss Confident tells her it would be wonderful if they could go together because she doesn't like going to conferences alone and would love to have a second set of ears to pick up ideas. She says, "I am not as detail orientated as you, and your skills would be so helpful."

Misty quickly picks up her jaw, so the pizza doesn't roll right out onto the table. In her head, she is thinking, "What? She thinks I can do something better than her? She is uncomfortable going alone?" Misty agrees to go along even though inside she feels inferior and knows she will feel substandard all weekend. Much to her surprise, they begin a friendship that forever changes her life. She learns that inside Miss Confident is really a human being much like herself, but who has chosen to accept herself and work toward developing her confidence every day. She makes the choice to appear confident even in her times of insecurity.

Add the Bling action step: Never let them see you sweat. No matter how afraid or doubtful you are, always go forward with courage. Confidence is gained through repeated practice.

Bling is having fear and doubt but pushing through with confidence, never allowing your inner critical voice to rule.

Blah is convincing yourself that you are not good enough.

Positive Self-Image

"When you look in the mirror, does your reflection show what you practice?"

Confidence begins with the image you have of yourself. You want to see yourself as in control, a leader who knows what they are doing, in charge of their life. This is the type of person you and others want to be around. It is crucial to feel comfortable with yourself. This may sound crazy, but if the internal image you have is not that of power and acceptance, you will not have any influence on yourself and certainly not on others.

A sustained image of control, confidence, and love will lead you to victory.

Your self-image is how you talk, look, and think, your capacity to learn and achieve. The image you need to create first is the one in the mirror; if you like that one, all the others will fall in place.

A positive self-image is when you look in the mirror and see your beautiful eyes, or a warm smile staring back at you, not a tired face or a heavier figure than you like. You admire your beautiful complexion, not focusing on a wrinkle. You see a strong, kind, compassionate soul with unlimited gifts and talents, and you remind yourself that seeing inside yourself is more important than the image in the mirror.

Blah to Bling example: Beth had allowed herself to slip. She began overeating which led to weight gain, so she got a little sloppy in her dressing style, trying to hide the extra pounds, and avoided the scale and the mirror because she couldn't face herself. If she looked, she might have to face reality, so instead she avoided it all together. This ate away at her inside and the longer she allowed it to go on, the worse it became. Soon she was so uncomfortable with herself that she avoided all social events, only going into public when she had to. When friends stopped by to try to cheer her up and encourage her to go out with them, she demeaned herself, making negative comments and wallowing in her sorrows until they quit visiting.

One day she was feeling sorry for herself as she was watching TV. Flipping through the channels, she came across a woman on a talk show describing her experiences which were much like Beth's. She explained how one day she looked in the mirror and didn't even know the person staring back at her. She began to talk to herself, asking her own image, "Who are you?" Surprisingly, the image staring back at her said, "I am whoever you wish me to be. I am a wonderful person waiting to be brought forward. All it takes is one little choice: to decide to accept me." She was shocked at how staring into her own eyes and asking questions brought emotions and answers to the surface. She made it a daily practice and soon feel in love with the person in her mirror and was amazed at how the world now viewed her. Beth had an ah-hah moment—

why would anyone want to be around her if she didn't even want to be around herself? She begins at once to build the image of herself she wanted the world to see.

Add the Bling action step: Look yourself in the mirror daily and tell yourself you are a wonderful person, and all is possible because you believe in you. This may sound crazy and will be uncomfortable at first, but if you make this a daily habit, you will be astonished at the changes you will see in yourself. You would encourage others, so why not yourself?

Bling is accepting yourself, loving who you are, and encouraging yourself to be your best.

Blah is judging yourself, talking down to that inner you.

Gratitude

*"When you awake each day, be grateful you are alive,
you can breathe, think, love, and enjoy."*

Gratitude is life's most rewarding possession.

Realizing what you already have is the first step in receiving all you want. Bling is being happy with what you have, even during the struggle to gain more or become better. You should be careful to remember that more is not always better. When you allow yourself to get caught up in the race for more, bigger, better, this drains you and ruins your self-esteem. It is like the elusive carrot dangling out in front of you just out of reach—you keep lunging at it but keep coming up short. Bling is embracing what you have and working toward increasing its value instead of always wanting more. You can never have more unless you appreciate what you already have. The grass is always greener if watered; you just need to take better care of your own.

True gratitude is finding your husband's clothes scattered all over the floor and being grateful you have a husband. Or being in accident and saying, "Thank God I'm OK, even though my car is totaled." Gratitude is not liking your job but being grateful you have one.

Take time today to cherish what you have—it could be gone tomorrow.

There is nothing wrong with wanting to improve yourself, but you must first appreciate all the great gifts you have. When the glass is half empty, many times it is because of all the holes left in the sides allowing the good to seep away. If you do not appreciate what you already have, your glass will never be full because you are too busy trying to fill your glass, allowing the blessings in your life to seep through the cracks. It will be a never-ending rat race until you appreciate what you already have right before you. Bling is approaching life with an open heart of gratitude, giving you a secure container to hold what you have so you can progress to overflowing your cup with more blessings. Acknowledging the good in your life is the foundation of all abundance.

Blah to Bling example: There is a story about a man who decided he needed to find his pot of gold. He woke one morning, got dressed, and walked through his kitchen where a wonderful breakfast was being cooked. His beautiful wife greeted him with a warm smile and his children exclaimed with excitement, "Good morning Daddy, we love you!"

He told them he had to go find his pot of gold, so his wife handed him his lunch, wished him well, and told him they would be there waiting anxiously for his return. He thought to himself, "Can they not see that happiness is out there for me to find and I will not be returning?" and he started on his journey.

Every evening when he took off his shoes, he would point them in the direction in which he was traveling so he would not lose his way, and each morning he would slip into his shoes as they sat and off he would go to find his riches.

One night, there was a loud noise that startled him, and he jumped up to see what it was, knocking his shoes. Finding nothing, he straightened his shoes and went back to sleep. In the morning, he once again slipped into his shoes and continued his journey.

Several days later, he arrived at a quaint home with a picket fence that had a squeaky gate needing some oil, and he thought to himself, "This is much like mine at home." From inside, he heard the laughter of children, and smelled the aroma of good food cooking inside. He swung open the door and the children came running to him with open arms and his wife gave him a big kiss and said, "Sit down honey, your dinner will be ready soon. We missed you." He settled in his chair and thought to himself, "Heaven at last. I am very grateful for my pot of gold."

Add the Bling action step: Each day, take time to be thankful for all that you already have. If you are upset or disappointed, first think of at least three things in your life you are grateful for, and you will soon not be as upset or disappointed.

Bling is appreciating all the blessings you already have, no matter how small or imperfect they are.

Blah is finding fault in all you have, never taking time to realize just how blessed you already are.

Persistence

"Our greatest weakness lies in giving up."

Endure until you succeed.

Success is progression toward our goals, pure perseverance, and consistent action. It is not an event, a destination, or a final achievement. Results do not always manifest immediately, but you must continue anyway, knowing in your heart you will succeed even if the present circumstances seem otherwise. Small daily victories toward your dreams are what make up a successful, prosperous, and happy life. You cannot fail if you keep going; failure only happens when you lay down or quit. Rome wasn't built in a day and neither is success—it is an ongoing journey and you must learn to enjoy the ride. Consistency is not a gift; it is a choice and is highly underrated. The harder you work for something, the greater you feel when you achieve it. It is a huge surge to your confidence.

If you decide to go to college, you don't go for one day and get your diploma, that's it, you're done. You will need to go to classes for months and years depending on what you choose to be. There will be exam after exam; some will go well, and others will not but you don't quit at the first sign of failure. You simply keep going to class, studying for another test and studying some more, passing one here, barely getting by that one there. But you keep pushing because you know each day you are getting a little closer to your career.

Don't stop when you're tired. Stop when you're done.

Never give up when things don't go as planned or you meet with failure or the naysayers tell you it can't be done. Have the perseverance to stick to it; relentlessly moving forward will lead to your success. Consistent action will always lead you to your dreams. If you stay true to yourself and your dreams, values, and passions you will achieve them.

Blah to Bling example: When climbers decide to take on Mount Everest, they don't just set out one day and climb to the top. It takes much preparation. When they arrive at base camp, they must acclimatize themselves to the altitude before going any higher, which can take weeks, and then they climb only to a designated point each day. They keep their eye on the goal, getting to the top, but they know that it will require many steps progressing toward that achievement. Although they know many climbers never make it and some never return, they are willing to fight and endure till they succeed. Even those who do not reach the top or return are all still a success because they gave it their all. Success is not reaching your goals, it is the progression toward them.

Add the Bling action step: Ask yourself daily, "What action can I take to move me closer to my goals?" and then take that action. Never discount the smallest of tasks as unimportant—everything counts.

Bling is pushing your way through even if you don't see a way, casting aside the limiting beliefs, and finding a way to make it happen.

Blah is giving up, or haphazardly pursuing your goals without conviction.

Decisiveness

"One single mental move will solve enormous problems in an instant: decision."

Decision is the start of discipline.

D ecide right where you are now what you want. Don't give it another thought, don't concern yourself with the how, just begin to work toward your dreams, charge them with enthusiasm, and you will be amazed at how things begin to fall into place. Change is hard, but knowing the payoff is more valuable to you than the current results you are experiencing can help lessen the discomfort. Remember, half the battle is making the decision to change and change gets easier with practice. We repeat behaviors that make us feel good in the moment. You are always going to repeat behaviors that make you feel good until you decide that feeling uncomfortable to achieve the unthinkable is possible and worth it.

For instance, you make the decision to get up early to work out. When the alarm goes off that first morning, you are not going to automatically spring to your feet. It will probably go more like, "It's dark, I'm tired, what was I thinking?" You will need to remind yourself that you made this decision to get in shape because you don't want to live with bad health. That having extra energy will allow you to get more done each day. It will be easy to tell yourself you will start tomorrow, but if you wish to accomplish your goals, you need to stick with your decision and remember the rewards of doing so are far greater than staying in bed.

Indecision creates internal conflict and disintegration and dominates your entire life.

If you cannot make a decision promptly once you have all the necessary facts, you cannot be depended upon to carry through any decision you make. The point of a decision is taking action—just deciding will not get the task done.

Blah to Bling example: David grew up in a good home with loving parents who did their best to guide him. He made good grades because he came right home from school and got his studies done before he ate dinner and enjoyed doing his favorite activities afterward.

He met some new friends at school and they started stopping by the local arcade on the way home. As time went on, he started coming home later and later until he was missing dinner with his family and was completely neglecting his studies. Before long he had given up his hobbies and all his time was spent with his new friends.

One day, one of the boys decided to shoplift in the local store. The owner caught the boys and they were all were arrested because no one would tell which one did it. This was the start of very many ugly events to come in David's life which led to more crime, drugs, and alcohol.

The pastor was visiting him after getting out of jail once again when David told him, "I don't understand how this all happened." The pastor explained that our decisions either keep us on the right path or can completely sidetrack us. They determine who we are and the results, circumstances, and situations in our lives. It doesn't seem like a big deal to let little things go, but before we know it, we have lost our way.

David thought all night about what he had said, and the next morning he decided he would develop his discipline, so he could get his life back on track. He outlined his plan: there were many things he had to decide to give up and things he would need to do that he didn't want to, but he knew it was the only way. To this day, when David wants to sway from his discipline, he reminds himself of the consequences of not following the decisions he has made. This keeps him grateful for the things he has, and he no longer treats his self-discipline as something he must do; he is glad to do it because he made the decision to.

Add the Bling action step: When there is a decision to be made, ask yourself, "What will I gain or what pain must I endure from this decision?"

Bling is weighing the consequences and then deciding and moving forward, never looking back or questioning yourself.

Blah is not considering what your decision may bring or what not deciding may lead to. This leads to others deciding our fate for us.

Self-Motivation

"

Others can inspire me but only I can change me."

Push yourself, because no one else is going to do it for you. If you wish to move beyond your current circumstance, who you are, or what you have, you will need to be motivated to make changes. You cannot just sit back and expect success to fall in your lap. You need to fuel your motivation to accomplish change; others may inspire you, but in the end, you will have to be your own cheerleader. You cannot rest on the sidelines of the life of your dreams; you must be willing to put in the work, effort, and time to gain what you want. No one owes you anything. Acknowledge and accept that, because you will never be motivated until you do. You will get back in direct proportion what you put out; don't fool yourself into thinking otherwise.

Motivating yourself means learning a new skill so you can get a promotion at work, not waiting for your company to provide it. It means eating an apple a day to stay healthy instead of waiting for you doctor to give you ultimatums if you don't. It is making choices to better your life, putting in the work even when you would rather do something else.

The door to opportunity is marked "PUSH."

Blah To Bling

You will need motivation to achieve your desires. If what you want to do does not excite you, stop now and find something else. If you are not passionate about your goal, your motivation will struggle and eventually die. Remember, motivation must come from within—others can help light the fire, but you will have to keep it fueled.

Blah to Bling example: Valerie spent her life blaming others for all her misfortunes. She wanted to go to college, but her parents didn't have the money, so she didn't go, and now she is broke and working a dead-end job. She expects others to give her things and help her out because she has been dealt a bad hand. It's not her fault everything in her life has gone wrong, it's their fault.

Her brother who grew up in the same circumstances has a different outlook. He knew his parents couldn't put him through college, so he started doing any odd jobs he could at a very young age. When all his friends were playing ball, he was working because he had a dream in his heart and no one was going to keep it from him. He worked hard to get good grades, so he could earn grant money, he worked two jobs all through college, and when finished he had mounting student debt, but he never complained. When things were tough—and that was often—he focused on the dreams he had, and this motivated him to push through. He never blamed anyone, so he succeeded.

Add the Bling action step: Constantly ask yourself, "What do I want to do, why, and what do I need to do to get it?" Remind yourself no one owes you anything; you must go out and get it.

Bling is finding ways to motivate yourself, not waiting for an outside force to do it. Motivation is an inside game.

Blah is allowing yourself to bounce around with no direction, expecting someone to push you.

Patience

"It is easier to keep the momentum going than it is to keep starting over."

Have patience on the long road.

P atience is a virtue, you have been told. It is true that greater rewards come to those who wait instead of settling. Did you have dreams of a career that required many years of college but allowed yourself to settle for a job much less fulfilling because you could begin sooner? Did you want a meaningful relationship with someone who shared your dreams but got tired of looking, or were lonely, so you settled for who was available at the time? Do not fall victim to instant gratification; you must be able to envision the future you desire. Keep your eye on the target, on what you truly want, not what is in front of you right now. Appealing distractions can lead you astray. Rainbows blind you to the pot of gold at the end—you see the beauty in front of you and settle, never searching any further—however, rainbows last only a short time; they soon fade away and the black clouds of Blah return.

What controls your attention controls your life.

The reasons your dreams elude you is that you let others discourage you, falling into the habit of settling for average, allowing past disappointments to hinder you, and settling for a lack of confidence in your dreams and even the lack of imagination to dream. You must be willing to fight for your dreams. Inspiration gets you started, but then fatigue sets in. You never intended on giving up, but you settled here and there, your life became mundane, average, and Blah, and before you knew it, your dreams slipped away.

Settling robs you of your confidence and creates a life of Blah. Keep your eye on the rewards you will receive if you keep following the path to your dreams. It's a never-ending journey but one worth taking. Decide what you want, what you are willing to give for it, set your mind to it, and go get your dreams.

Blah to Bling example: I always wanted to be an architect. I spent my life drawing homes and designing plans. When I graduated high school, I was faced with many years of college ahead of me before I could start making money. All my friends were going to trade school because it was a lot less time and they could be making money more quickly. Although I had dreamed of being an architect my whole life and felt I would love it, the pull of faster results tugged at me. I settled for going to beauty school because it was only nine months until I could get my license and make some money to buy a car. Although I ended up owning a very successful business, I had let instant gratification steal my dreams. I didn't give up, I'm still creating my dreams, but I now keep a close watch on letting instant gratification blind me again.

Add the Bling action step: Before you make a choice, stop and ask yourself: "Is this what I really want or am I settling for instant gratification?" It's OK to be flexible and use plan B to build plan A, but don't allow it to become a permanent substitution.

Bling is making the choices needed to achieve your ultimate desires.

Blah is giving in to the moment and giving up on your dreams.

Compassion

"Everything that irritates us about others can lead us to an understanding of ourselves."

Compassion is a state of constant giving.

Strive to treat everyone as you want to be treated yourself; make others feel how you would like to feel. This attitude brings fullness, meaning, and purpose to your life. The feeling you receive when you make someone's life better is the one of the greatest confidence builders. The simplest of gestures accomplish this: a warm smile, a compliment, words of encouragement, saying thank you, a card, a text, or better yet, a call for no reason. Everyone has their own agendas that can make them appear rude or mean, but this is actually a front for some pain they are suffering. Make it your goal to create the world you wish to see one action or gesture at a time. Every kind act, no matter how small, will add value and joy to the world. You will receive ten times the value of any you give.

Compassion is packing someone's lunch even though you would rather sleep in. It is when you have limited funds and you buy something for someone else instead of yourself. It's going to the party of a friend who is counting on you when you really want to do something else. It is forgiving someone who has wronged you.

Compassion for others gives you charisma.

When you can give all you know freely so that you may help others advance, you show confidence in yourself and your abilities. We all have some knowledge to share and when we spread it, it becomes wisdom. Keeping things from others so that you may know more will only destroy confidence, not build it. When you share a good idea or tip and you see it helps someone else prosper, your self-esteem will grow. We build ourselves by building others. Remember you have gifts and talents that the world needs, so don't be afraid to share them. Share the gift of your best self; watch the possibilities unfold before you, and your gifts, purpose, and direction will reveal themselves.

Blah to Bling example: Sam was an attorney. He loved his job but really wanted to move into the senior position, so he worked long hours perfecting his skills. A new attorney who was young and eager and had a lot to learn joined the firm. Sam took him under his wing and taught him all he had learned over the years. He was very proud of his progress and felt he himself had grown through his teachings as well.

When the senior position became available, it was in fact granted to the very person he had trained. Most people would have been bitter and resentful, but Sam was proud of him and had no hard feelings. He thought that if the company chose him, then he was the better choice, and it would be wrong to end a good friendship. Others in the office did not share Sam's kindness and slighted the new partner, which of course caused tension for him. Sam once again shared his wisdom: he explained that their bad behavior was simply jealousy rearing its ugly head and had nothing to do with him. He gave the new partner a pat on the back and a warm smile, and urged him to not let them discourage him. Sam is truly a shining example of charisma and it payed off in many rewards through his life, even though it didn't in this situation.

Add the Bling action step: Ask yourself, "When was the last time I did something for someone without any thought to how it will benefit me? Do I turn the other cheek and take the high road when someone is rude, and I would like to respond back the same way?"

Bling is always putting yourself in the shoes of others and then treating them as yourself, even if they don't return the kind gesture.

Blah is responding to others in a rude manner when they are rude to you. It's keeping ideas to yourself and not helping others to give yourself the advantage.

Independence

"Encourage and influence others. Build their character and you build them."

Lead by creating independence, not dependence.

You need to shine the spotlight on others, share recognition, and refocus on what others have done or have to offer. You earn success based on your service to others, not at the expense of others. You cannot manage others by telling them what to do; instead, inspire them to do their best—that is the sign of a true leader. You must put yourself in their shoes and try to view the world though their eyes to truly inspire them.

As a leader you help your child with their school project, offering guidance and encouragement, but resist the urge to do it yourself because it is quicker. Or you are part of a big project at work, and although you are to work as a team, you find yourself doing most of the work, staying late when others have left and coming in a little earlier to meet the deadline. Even though the supervisor gives equal rewards to all, you smile and relish in the glory with your team.

Give recognition: the smallest of gestures make the biggest difference.

Self-worth comes from within and you have no reason to try to steal the show. This mindset radiates humility.

93

Others are attracted to you because of how you make them feel, not by how much you have to prove. When others perceive you as confident, not conceited, they are more likely to connect with you and act on your words. Try to lead others to find their own path, independence, and gifts, not to follow you. Leaders give others the courage to act and to make their own decisions; they don't control them.

Blah to Bling example: Samantha was the manager of a retail store. Her duties were to grow revenue, manage the workers, and build the store's reputation. She was always giving orders to the employees, trying to get them to work harder and treat customers better. Her approach was controlling, and she was quick to take credit for any progress. The employees did not like or respect her, so turnover was a constant problem. The corporation decided to bring in another manager to see if they could discover why the store wasn't succeeding.

The new manager, Julie, came in with a different approach. She asked the employees for their ideas and encouraged them to offer suggestions on how to improve the store. At first, they were shocked and felt it must be a trick, but they soon warmed up to her way of thinking. Their trust in her grew, as did revenues. Corporate was very impressed and congratulated Julie on all her success, but she was quick to explain that the others were just as much a part of the success as her. She explained that she simply encouraged them to be their best, guided them when needed, and strove to create a team atmosphere. This gave the team a sense of belonging, and they began to feel like they were a part of the corporation, not just employees. This sense of ownership in turn changed how they treated the customers because they felt like they were their customers as well.

Add the Bling action step: Ask yourself, "Do I hold others up or push them down with my actions and attitude?" If the answer is not helping others to be more, start today by looking for ways to become a better leader.

Bling is being a leader, not a control freak. It's showing confidence in others' abilities to achieve and guiding them to be their best selves.

Blah is trying to control others, putting them down, or making them dependent upon you.

Courage

"To conquer yourself, you must believe you can."

Belief trumps fear.

Do not let fear hold you back; if you don't try, you cannot succeed. Low-key change helps your brain avoid the fight-or-flight response, so you remain creative. Big goals trigger fear and our fears govern us. Boldness has genius, power, and magic in it but is more easily achieved if you begin with smaller steps leading to the big, bold and powerful goals. Whatever you can do or dream you can do, begin today. The more you tackle your fears, the less powerful they become, so face them head on with courage. Your thinking is not clear if you allow yourself to be in a state of fear; your emotions are out of control and you feel out of control. The fearful become fearless the more they push through their fears.

Courage is when you are faced with a big decision and you have no idea how it will turn out. You want to start that new business venture, but where will you get the money? How will you pay the bills you already have, how will you get customers, what will others say when you walk away from your current job to take a chance? Although it scares you to death, you step forward. Your gut says, "Run, turn back, this is too scary," but you move forward one day at a time because in your heart you know this is what you want, that you can and will overcome the challenges that lie ahead of you.

The greatest test of courage is to bear defeat without losing heart, to move from one failure to another with enthusiasm. Confidence is not the absence of fear, but challenging it head on, accepting your fears and doing it anyway.

Curiosity allows possibilities and keeps us fresh. To be curious is to be optimistic.

Be optimistic. Have no doubt in your ability to do the things you want to do—although you may not know how to do it today, you know you are capable. Know you can do it and you will; it has nothing to do with where you are right now. Your abilities are not a thing given at birth but rather a process of growth. You can become anything you wish and knowing this is what will set you free to be who you want to be. You will undeniably be what you think, so it's very important to be optimistic with your thoughts.

Courage is when you seek out others to teach you something new. Maybe you decided you wanted to learn to play the piano. You have never even touched the keys before, so what makes you think you can? You start asking questions, visit a piano store, introduce yourself to the pianist at church. The more inquiries you make, the more excited you become because you realize that they too started out with no idea how to play; they simply gained the skill.

Nothing can keep you from the things you want except yourself. You may be scared, but move forward with courage and belief. Believe that life is worth living and your belief will create that fact. Get comfortable being uncomfortable.

Extraordinary things happen only when we believe in ourselves enough to take risks.

Growth and change do not happen in your comfort zone; you must stretch your boundaries to grow. Things may seem intimidating at first, but the more you do it, the more comfortable it gets. It's like when new shoes are too tight—the more you wear them, the better they feel. Going beyond your normal limits can be scary; just remember you don't have to be great to start, you just must get started. What matters is that you do it to the best of your ability at that time and will continue to commit to improving. If you stay in your own backyard, you cannot find advancement; the limiting fence will always hold you back.

Pessimism leads to weakness, optimism to power.

When faced with something you don't want to do because it seems scary or hard, or may even seem downright impossible, do it anyway. If you fall on your face, pick yourself up and go at it again.

Blah to Bling example: There were two sisters who both had dreams, and both carefully planned out the things they needed to do to accomplish them. The difference was one jumped in with both feet and went to work on achieving her dreams while the other continued to procrastinate. She wasn't going to start before everything was just right because she didn't want to make mistakes. It is true that the one who jumped in made plenty of mistakes and had some failures and disappointments, but she accomplished her dreams and continues to build new ones every day. The other—well, she never made a mistake, but she did fail and suffered disappointments because she never took action. She suffered the greatest failure of all: she never achieved anything because she never tried.

Add the Bling action step: Ask yourself what the worst that can happen is and decide if the fear you have is worth conquering to accomplish what you want.

Bling is not letting our fears keep us from what we want. It is having the courage to resist and master fear.

Blah is allowing your fears to steal your dreams, and sitting on the sidelines because you fear life.

Clarity

"Lack of clarity and direction creates failure."

You can't hit the bull's-eye if you don't know where to aim.

To truly own your life, you must be clear about who you are and why you do what you do. Clarity is the root of true confidence; knowing what you want is the first step to getting it. If you are not clear on what you want from life, it is certain you will never get it. You can't set goals, plan of action, or design your road map if you don't know where it is you are going.

Don't question your abilities when deciding what you want or how to get it, just know you can and you will achieve it, and set forth toward its achievement. The more action you take toward your target, the clearer the journey becomes. Clarity comes from engagement, not thought alone; you cannot hit a target that you do not have. To be effective, you must focus, decide on your priorities, and channel your energies into the tasks before you that will lead you where you choose to go. Once you figure out who you are and what you love, the rest all seems to fall into place as long as you keep the faith.

Clarity is when you set your sights on getting that new car—you don't have the money right now, maybe you don't even have a driver's license yet, but none of that matters. You are going to have it. You dream about it, picture it in your mind, get the brochures. You know every color choice and option available. When you mention it to others, they scoff at your wish. They say "You can't afford that. What do you need that car for? There are others much cheaper." But you pay no attention. You know exactly want you want down to the last detail and no matter what, it will be yours someday.

You think you know what you want, but do you really or do you want what you have been told you want? Is what you want something you have just been programmed to want by someone else, for instance, going to college, getting married, or the career path you are on? Many times, you are influenced by what others want or what you are "supposed to do." You are told to want these things over and over until you yourself start to believe it, and once you have them, you are miserable, because deep down they are not what you wanted, they are what you settled for.

When you are young, you are supposed to know what you want to be for the rest of your life. Right out of high school, you are pressured to make very important decisions based on no knowledge or experience other than what is being impressed upon you. You are so young; how can you possibly know what you really want? So most of the time, you set out on a life of someone else's ideals. They don't mean harm, they feel they are doing what's best for you, that's how it went for them, and it's the only way they know. The problem is you are given someone else's map and it will not take you to your destination, but to theirs.

One day, you wake up and say to yourself, "How did I get here? My life is not at all what I want, but now I'm stuck." You are never stuck. You always have the option to choose to start again; it's never too late to pursue your dreams. You may have even had a wonderful life, known what you wanted, and gone after it and achieved it with success, but now things have changed. This will happen because you are always evolving, and what was once important to you may no longer be. Just design a new map.

Knowing what you want, like most things, is a journey, and the more you step forward, the clearer the path with become. However, if you don't get started, it gets fuzzier with the passing of every day until you are completely blind. As you work toward getting a clear focus on your dreams, you will evolve and change. Clarity comes by constantly adjusting the lens that you look through.

Blah to Bling example: Imagine going on vacation. You carefully pack all the things you will need. You are very excited and can't wait. You jump out of bed the morning your vacation starts, grab your coffee, and out the door you go.

You jump in the car, start it up, and you sit there. You never selected a destination or got a map, so you have no idea where you are going or how to get there.

You decide you will start driving, so off you go, turning left then right and left again. You drive around aimlessly for hours. You would stop to ask directions, but you don't know where to ask directions to. How can anyone help you if you don't even know where you are going? After a while you are tired, frustrated, and completely lost, so you hit the navigation for home and it safely delivers you right back where you started. If you had just begun with the most important thing—deciding where you want to go—your navigation would have taken you there, and if you got lost, you could have asked for help along the way.

Add the Bling action step: Write down your goals—if you don't, they're merely dreams—and read them three times a day. Clarity comes from constant reminders.

Bling is getting clear on what you want and then putting together your plan for getting it.

Blah is lack of direction with no conviction to gain it.

Imagination

"Dreams, imagination, same thing—both can destroy ordinary."

Your imagination can either keep you stuck or lead you to new territory—which will it be? You cannot let your current circumstance dictate your future; you must use your imagination to create what you presently do not have. That is the problem with most: they cannot see beyond their current thoughts. What is real to them is only what they can see with their eyes.

True vision is not through your eyes, it is through your thoughts and imagination; you must learn to see beyond what you are currently experiencing. You must first see in your mind what you really want and who you wish to be before you can bring those things into physical being. Everything around you grew out of someone's imagination. You have one too, and you must learn to use it. Envision your dreams, passions, and desires so vividly that they are real to you, and then act as if they are already present.

Imagination is when you have a circumstance in your life such and an illness, unfavorable working conditions, or maybe a relationship. You see in your future a healthy you, or creating a new business enterprise or better job, or a loving and cooperative relationship. Although the current situation is not what you want, you can see beyond it to a vision you dream of, knowing you can create it.

Nothing expands possibilities like unleashed imagination. Small thinking limits achievement.

The only limitations you have are the ones you place upon yourself, so stop being your own worst enemy. Think outside the box, the sky is the limit, imagine big. Anything you dream up can be yours for the taking, but first you must see it in your mind.

Blah to Bling example: Walt Disney World, "A place where dreams come true," is where Mr. Disney's imagination came to life. If you visit it, you will see true imagination becoming reality everywhere you look. Put yourself in his shoes: when he started, none of those things existed. He created them in his mind and then brought them into being. Nothing of its kind had ever been created before, so imagine the naysayers he faced. A grown man drawing cartoon characters, bringing them to life, and making a park—he had lost his mind.

This is probably just one of the comments made, but he could see beyond his present state because he had a vivid imagination and vision. You must remind yourself when you see amazing, astonishing things that they all were created by someone's imagination. It all starts with a thought, backed with courage.

Add the Bling action step: Ask yourself what things you would do if no one, including yourself, told you that you couldn't. Begin today to view the world as a child—they don't know they can't do something, so they just try. Using your imagination is not just for children.

Bling is thinking and creating your wildest dreams. Imagine your future through a child's eyes where there are no limitations.

Blah is allowing yourself to live your life through someone else's imagination, limiting your dreams because of your lack of imagination.

Positive Attitude

"We create our own reality based on our attitude."

Attitudes are contagious.

Your attitude—your personality, values, and characteristics—determines your life. You get up every day and put it on: you choose whether you are putting on the Blah or the Bling. Your attitude is how others perceive you; it's all of your thoughts, beliefs, and perspectives wrapped up in one package. No one can see your shining personality, values, or characteristics if they cannot see beyond your attitude. It is your outermost impression, and it speaks loud and clear before you even realize it.

Thinking positive is all a part of your attitude. Once you replace negative thoughts with positive ones, you'll start having positive results. Negative thoughts push away your creativity, passion, and joy. Positive thinking attracts other positive people to you, and negative thoughts bring negative people to you—like attracts like. Negative thinking leads to bad attitudes; both are highly contagious diseases, easily contracted and easily spread.

Each day, you need to decide that no matter what life throws at you, you are going to remain positive. When you allow a bad attitude, you give up your control: you are reacting instead of acting. Giving up your control creates a snowball effect and everything in your day heads in the wrong direction.

Having a positive attitude is getting a flat tire and looking at it as "It could be worse, I could have been in an accident." Or not getting the promotion you wanted but focusing on how there will always be another opportunity and maybe the next one will be even better. Positive attitude is looking at losing the game as an actual chance to bond and create new relationships with your team members during the battle.

Nothing can bring you peace but yourself.

Never allow others to take away your control, and never stoop to their level. The only one who can take away your power is you. When you are feeling hurt, jealous, or angry, you must realize resorting to evil and devious means will steal your confidence because you forfeit your control. Confidence comes from having control over your emotions and thoughts; when you are in possession of them, no one can steal your power. The minute you give in to their actions and react, you have given them control. Always act in accordance with who you are and never become a mirror of others' actions.

Expect criticism from others, especially as you strive to be your best, become more, and succeed more. It is all part of choosing to be Exceptional and stepping away from the tribe of average thinkers. They will view you as a threat, but don't allow it to rattle you—they have the same right to be better, but choose to settle for less. Don't criticize their choices; live by your ideals, not others' personalities.

Blah to Bling example: You get up late and in your haste, you spill your coffee all over yourself and now you have to pick out another outfit which upsets you because you hate everything in your closet, all 100 outfits.

Out the door you go, and you drop your keys in a mud puddle because it's raining, of course. Some idiot in front of you wants to drive the speed limit—doesn't he know you are late?—so you have a few choice words and gestures for him. Then someone else cuts you off in traffic and off you go on a rant. Your mom calls to tell you something and you nearly bite her head off.

You get to work late so you blow past everyone without saying hello, and when you get to your desk, you have a slew of calls and emails, all bad news. Can't someone give you a break? The whole day is a barrage of unpleasant events, nothing goes right, and you grow more irate as the day goes on. Each encounter fuels your bad attitude into a full-blown inferno.

Congratulations, you have settled for being less than your best, Blah!

Every person you come in contact with represents the opportunity to act with character or react with insecurity.

If you put on the right attitude, your day would look more like this: OK, so you're running behind. It's not the end of the world; take a deep breath and just move through your morning routine at a slightly faster pace.

Look at yourself in the mirror and say, "It's going to be the best day of my life." It truly will be if you decide that you will recognize the small miracles all around you instead of the evil. Pick your outfit and know you look great. Don't let those self-defeating voices have a say in it.

When you step outside, think, "Great! Some rain to water my flowers so I don't have to later." When you get behind the gentleman who is probably saving your life by setting a slower pace, smile and say, "Everything happens for a reason. At least I won't get a ticket." When you get cut off, assume that person has an emergency and their intention was not to be rude, and wish them safe travels in their haste.

When Mom calls, wish her a good morning and be grateful you have a mom. She may have something very important to say, or maybe not, but either way give her a minute—she gave you life after all. Although you may need to move swiftly past your coworkers, smile, wish them a good day, and say, "Running behind, sorry! Let's catch up later." When the phone calls and emails look intimidating, take another deep breath and vow to find a solution to each one. Don't look at them as issues, but as a puzzle to solve, which you can do because you are Exceptional—Bling!

Before you know it, someone brings you a cup of coffee with a smile. The next call is a kind person thanking you for all you do. You get an email with good news. At lunch, when you realize you didn't have time to make yours, you decide to take a walk to get something, which gets you some fresh air, and it even ceases to rain long enough for you to go.

I am not saying that these events will happen just like that, but if you make up your mind to be positive, happy, and grateful, your entire day will turn out quite differently. You can make the sunshine and rainbows appear and find the pot of gold—it is always inside of us if we will just choose to look for it.

Add the Bling action step: When you find yourself in a situation that is less than kind, treat all those involved as you wish to be treated, not as you are being treated.

Bling is choosing to be your best when faced with adversity, criticism, and pain.

Blah is allowing yourself to react to emotions provoked by others' actions.

Character

"Be an incredible example. Do things the right way, without cheating or compromising—that is character."

Take complete control of your character to become unstoppable.

You must always be a quality brand. Be a person of high values, principles, and honesty; this earns respect. Do not be all talk and no action; be the type of person you admire. Know your values and always strive to be what you say you are. Keep your word with yourself and others. Your reputation is based on what you say you will do, what you value, and how well you keep those promises. If you don't keep promises, it chips away at your self-esteem. If you say it, mean it and do it or keep quiet. Words are meaningless unless backed by integrity, character, and action. Character is developed and built by your choices, decisions, and values.

Character is when you have a friend who is being shunned or bullied and stepping up although it could bring the same treatment upon yourself. Or asking a friend to go to a concert with you because your boyfriend is busy, but when he has a change in plans, even though you really would like to go with him, keeping your commitment to your friend.

Being humble is the best way to brag.

It takes true humility to accept being wrong and to know it is OK. It does not make you a failure. You know what you are capable of and mistakes do not take away from that. At some point we are all wrong—I know that is hard to face, but it is a fact of life. Don't feel discouraged; it is all part of growing into your true self.

Humility is when you make a mistake that maybe no one even knows you made but you own up to it anyway. Maybe you said something about others that you shouldn't have, and it gets back to them, but they think it came from another party, and you tell them the truth.

Build others, not competition. There is room for everyone.

Confidence is not being afraid to ask questions. It yields hundreds of answers that will help you grow, it creates oxygen, it invites participation. If you act as if you know it all, others will check out on you. You will never be perfect—practice only makes us better, not perfect, because there is no such thing. We can at any moment step forward into further growth or backward into delusion, and you are truly deluding yourself more than anyone else when you think you cannot improve. Learning and progressing comes from listening to the answers to your questions—if you don't, you have wasted their time and yours. Knowledge comes through listening.

Never try to be better than anyone else, but never cease trying to be your best.

Never try to impress others; try to impress yourself and you will find happiness within you. Confidence means not trying to prove you are smarter or know more; there is no need to try to convince anyone of that. Listening to others not only helps you grow, but it shows compassion and interest in others. The quickest way to gain others' interest is to be interested in them. They don't care what you have to say, they care how you make them feel. When you make others feel important, understood, and interesting, they will gravitate toward you and your confidence will soar all because you kept quiet and listened instead of trying to prove your point.

Do you stretch the truth about something you have, or have done, trying to impress others? Maybe you claim you make more money than you do, or say you have more expensive belongings than you do because you feel yours may not measure up. Confidence is being proud of who you are or what you have without the need to place value in comparison to what others are or have.

Blah to Bling example: There were two auto salesmen, Andy and Henry, who both worked at a prominent dealership. Andy was very successful, and he made sure to point that out to everyone. He bragged about his car, his home, his fancy watch, and how much he knew about the business. Even though he never listened to anything his customers said, he still did well because he was very forceful. He struggled to find new clients, however, because no one ever returned to him: one experience was enough.

Henry, on the other hand, actually had twice as many sales as Andy, but no one knew that because he never mentioned it. At meetings he listened attentively so he could better his skills and knowledge. While Andy boasted about his recent sales, Henry kept an ear open in other departments as well as his own, so he could learn what to do and what not to do (and he learned plenty of not-to-dos from Andy). He would ask his customers what they wanted and listen for clues because many times he discovered what they wanted and what they truly needed were quite different. He would then make some suggestions based on what he heard, and they were thrilled because they left with a car that suited them, not the one the salesman wanted to sell them. Henry's success came from referrals and repeat business because he strove to be of value to his clients.

Add the Bling action step: Reflect on your actions, choices, and decisions of the day. Ask, "Was I a good example? One that I wish the world to see?" If not, commit to do better tomorrow, to learn from others, and to never assume you know it all.

Bling is walking your talk, being the person, you can look up to so others may too, and always remaining humble.

Blah is bragging, trying to prove you know more, saying one thing and doing another.

Accepting Responsibility

"Blame is an excuse to avoid responsibility"

Don't play blame games.

The Exceptional understand that when someone is trying to blame something on them, they are only trying to get the monkey off their own back. They may have not done their best and they know it, or may have not been truthful and are struggling with guilt. The easier way to escape those feelings is to blame someone else—which in this case happens to be you.

When you allow others to dump blame on you, you fuel the flames of insecurity. Ask yourself, "Did I have any part in this?" If not, move on and don't waste your energy on trying to remove the blame; you have nothing to prove. If, after very careful review, you find you may have been a part of the issue, take steps to correct it and move on.

Have you ever been in the situation where you did a job for someone and you know in your heart you did your best, however, they ask you for a discount which you cannot do and should not do? They then proceed to talk negatively about you to others, and you struggle with this because you know it is not your fault they choose to be dishonest. Did you let that drain your positivity and focus?

Blame hinders brainstorming and creates blamestorming. It zaps you of your creativity because you are wasting energy on reasons why it isn't your fault, trying to prove you're innocent. It creates an atmosphere of resentment because the emotion of hurt swirls around and around in your mind. Don't allow this pity party to go on. Stand up, take responsibility for your actions, and forget about false accusations.

You must decide you are responsible for all that happens in your life. I know you are thinking, "That's BS. It isn't my fault that blah blah blah happened..." If you keep thinking that way, you will never gain your confidence because you'll always have the mindset of a victim. It puts you on the defensive, and we never want to be in reaction mode. We want to act. No excuses, don't complain— either leave the situation, change it, or accept it for what it is and decide to learn from it and move on. All else is utter madness that will eat away at you and destroy your confidence.

Blah to Bling example: I heard a story on the news about Starbucks: they had decided to stop offering an incentive program which gave you a dime off a cup of coffee. The public went crazy, vowing to never go there again—how dare they make them pay the original price, it's unfair, blah, blah, blah. They placed all the blame on Starbucks instead of realizing that they received a temporary discount—no one promised them it was forever.

I personally love the Starbucks experience, and although I can get my mocha elsewhere for cheaper, I like theirs the best. I can't have one every day, but I enjoy the splurge. I don't believe they were ever about the value of the coffee; instead they are about quality, the Bling of the baristas. If you think they are too expensive, then shop elsewhere, but don't complain—you become the victim, which turns you into a whiner.

Be the Bling and stand strong in your choices and values. If saving cost is important, then go where you like, but don't berate others. You gain confidence in making a decision to do what you want for your own reasons, not someone else's. I guarantee many people watching that story avoided Starbucks for a while because the media told them to, but really, I don't like being told what to do. They probably really wanted their Starbucks, but the media said to boycott them, so they thought they had better follow along. The point is, if avoiding them is what you in your heart feel is right, then do it because you choose to.

We get so caught up in the beliefs that have been inflicted on us that we forget to think for ourselves. We are like the moth at the window: we want to go where we see a future, but allow an obstacle to prevent us from getting there. The world does not owe you, me, or anyone else. To be free, you must embrace this. We just keep banging our heads against the window pane because we don't take responsibility for our own actions, beliefs, and thoughts. Only when we accept that all is our choice can we find an opening to our desired future. When you do this, your confidence will soar.

Add the Bling step: The next time you find yourself being blamed for something you had nothing to do with, quietly smile and go about your business without a thought of arguing. If you are being blamed for something you may be responsible for, own it.

Bling is knowing that unsubstantiated blame is not yours to deal with. It is their issue to deal with; remove yourself from the situation.

Blah is going to battle with someone, placing blame on the wrong person, and trying to prove them wrong.

Section 3:
Habits

Our Habits Create Us

D aily rituals become your habits, and your habits create your life, your results, and you. It is very important to develop habits that will lead you where you want to go—bad habits seem easier to create and have a huge impact on your results. Take a good look at your current circumstances: like it or not, they are the accumulation of your habits. Confidence is a habit you create through your mindset, choices, and discipline. Viewing the creation of empowering habits as sacrifice is self-defeating, but seeing it as a choice that brings you toward your greater goals gives you strength and endurance to conquer.

Self-confidence is not developed by neglecting the small daily acts of self-discipline: they are what make you feel good about yourself. They create your confidence because you know you are doing your best every day, and nothing less. Self-mastery means putting off doing things of low priority, so you can get done the things that make a real difference.

To build the habits that will build the person you wish to be, you simply start making them a part of your daily routine. At first, it may seem like a struggle, however, the more you do them, the easier it will become. You will start to see changes in your results before you know it, and you will be amazed at how they happen much more easily than you thought.

Your routines, a sequence of repeated actions, the things you do without any thought, are what develop into your habits, which are automatic reactions. Breathing, believe it or not, is a habit—you subconsciously breathe without any thought. Routines begin with a little more thought than that, however: they are things you do and think automatically after repeated action. Your habits determine who you are, your results, and your circumstances. Look around your life and you can easily see what habits you have developed. To move beyond tolerating the average life, you need to adopt habits of the Exceptional life. To achieve excellence, to accomplish big things, you must develop the habits in little things. Excellence is not the exception; it is the prevailing attitude needed.

Once you have selected the person you want to create and the goals you want to achieve, and outlined the self-discipline you will need to get there, you must develop habits that will create your desired goals. You create your habits and then they create you: this is a simple truth and you must acknowledge this fact. We sometime delude ourselves into thinking we can't help what has happened to us or what our lives have become, but the reality is that we are our habits.

It isn't the big things you do that determine your destiny; that would be easy to spot. No, it is the smallest things you do every day that build or destroy you. They are the real danger because they are so small they go undetected.

You never eliminate a habit—at least not for long. The trick is developing new habits to replace the ones not leading you to your goals. This will take some thought because habits are like being on autopilot: you do things and don't even know you are doing them. You see the results from your habits but don't have a clue how they happened.

Start with who you want to be. Think about what habits you will need to develop to become that you. If you are not who you wish to be, then your habits must change because they have created that you. You may not know which habits you need, so role models are essential: study the things they do and don't do that create their results. Then work on developing their habits so you can create those results for yourself.

After you have selected the habits that you need to develop, look at the counterproductive habits you have. Once you begin the process of changing your negative habits to positive ones, it gets easier every day. You will be so happy with your new results that you will be anxious to create even more new habits. Be warned, becoming who you choose to be is very addictive. Create the habits that will lead you to your desired you, goals, and dreams, and they will take over and you no longer will have to think about it. One day, you will wake up that person and wonder how it was so easy when once you thought it was impossible.

Blah to Bling example: I wanted to be an entrepreneur, to work from home, and to write and develop programs to help others develop themselves. I knew I had to replace procrastination with action, so I developed the habit of action planning which structured my activities instead of allowing distractions to control me.

I created the habit of self-development every morning, getting up an hour earlier to fill my mind with the right thinking, reading and writing in my journal. I know you may be thinking, "I don't want to get up earlier, I am already tired enough." That's your choice. My choice was to create the me I wished to be, not the unfocused, unconfident, doubtful, worrying woman doing a job I didn't want to do. The habits I had created had determined my life and were keeping me there, so I had to kick them to the curb. Just so you know, once you start being the person you wish to be, energy will never be a problem again. It is living a life you don't like and stressing over the life you desire that sucks the life right out of you.

Take Care of Your Vessel

"Take good care of your body; it is the only place you have to live."

Decide to be young and to die at an old age.

You cannot be successful, confident, full of energy, vibrant, and positive unless you take care of your health. You must commit to caring for yourself. Your health affects every aspect of your life, and you need to accept that. You have to grow older in years, but you do not have to get old. You can choose to add life to every year, not just settle for tolerating aches and pains and giving up the things you love to do. You will get old if you don't take care of yourself; you can choose to eat things that nourish your body or you can choose junk that strips you of vital nutrients and puts foreign chemicals inside your body.

When you choose to eat the false impostors posing as food all around, you become dependent on others: the government, the healthcare system, and so much more. When you do not have your health, you are easily controlled because you are at their mercy. Decide you are not going to allow them to steal your dignity—take responsibility for your own health on your terms.

Proper care of yourself looks like eating whole foods as often as possible. By this I mean whole vegetables and fruits, grains, beans, lean proteins, unprocessed foods. Whole means as close to how nature made it as possible.

The more human participation involved, the less nutritious food becomes. If a packed product on the shelf that says real fruit added, put it down and go to the produce aisle for real fruit. If it offers numerous vegetable servings per container, look at how much sodium and chemicals come with them. Go to the produce aisle, where it's easy to count servings of vegetables based on how many vegetables you put in your cart.

Stay on the outside—of the store that is. The outside aisles of grocery stores are designed that way because they are closer to refrigeration, making them easier to stock. This means there aren't a ton of chemicals to preserve food here, unlike their counterparts in the internal parts of the store. Fresh and frozen are your best options. If you must rely on canned versions, be sure to rinse well.

You were not designed to eat chemicals, however a huge portion of the products all around you are just that: no nutritional value. Real food fuels your cells, organs, and functions of your body; when you allow yourself to live on laboratory-created products, you begin to break down and become ill. You cannot count on doctors to fix you; only you can through proper care and prevention of disease.

Give yourself a cheat from time to time, but remember cheating means behaving dishonestly, which means you are not being honest with yourself about this choice being healthy. That is OK on occasion, as long as you keep in mind this should not be your normal behavior and get back on track immediately.

Blah to Bling example: Mary was out of shape and overweight. She struggled with energy, ambition, and confidence, but felt she was in pretty good health otherwise. That's what she told herself anyway, because she avoided the doctor, so she would not have to face the test results, until one day she became ill.

What the doctor told her left Mary in a state of shock: she was a full-blown diabetic with high cholesterol and high blood pressure. The doctor told her she would need to begin at once taking medications to get these issues under control. Her doctor told her she should watch what she ate and exercise but gave her no real guidelines or help.

Mary had watched her mother die from diabetes complications, and she dreaded the pills, the shots, the pain, etc. She vowed she would not end up that way. She sought out the help of a friend who was a nutritionist and told the doctor to give her one month to improve before she would consider the medications. Her friend gave her guidelines for changing her food choices and explained that the food she ate was the key determining factor to her health. Mary immediately began making small changes every day toward improving her health. More of Mary's story is to come.

Add the Bling action step: Design your plan for becoming healthy, resolve to learn about nutritious foods, make exercise a habit, and don't count on any magic pills.

Bling is taking responsibility for your health, not leaving it to chance.

Blah is thinking the poor choices you are making don't affect your health.

Exercise

"Save your life: commit to exercise as a priority."

Exercise is a critical part of life.

When you neglect to exercise, that lack of discipline will translate into every area of your life. Activity is what makes your blood pump which leads to more mental clarity. Exercise is vital to confidence, self-esteem, and overall health. When you move more, you feel better and have more energy, stamina, and strength, and it gives you immediate gratification. The bonus is eventually you will see improvements in your physical condition. Exercise does so many great things for the mind, body, and soul, so move as much as you can. "Exercise is actually the single best thing you can do for your brain in terms of mood, memory, and learning," says Harvard Medical School psychiatrist John Ratey. "Even 10 minutes of activity changes the brain."

Confidence is gained through motion; movement clears your mind and energizes you. Exercise improves your attitude, spirit, and confidence as much as your physical health. According to a recent study in the Journal of Health Psychology, the act of exercising increases self-confidence. The good news is it doesn't matter how well you perform, or how long—the studies showed any exercise is better than none.

The results also showed the experience of exercise helps with depression because of the feeling of "euphoria" it can create. The more you move, the more you want to move, and that will lead you to a healthy body. When feeling Blah, go for a walk, do some yoga, lift some weights, and watch your confidence and energy soar. You don't have to run a marathon or work out for an hour; five minutes is enough to give you a boost. Chances are you will like the boost so much you will want more.

To add exercise to your day, simply moving more. Park a few more spaces away from the store and take the steps. Set a reminder to move at least once an hour. When you get back to your desk, your mind seems clearer and that problem you have been stumped on all morning magically has a resolution. After taking the steps, you feel energized and decide to do it more often, and the next thing you know, you are parking as far from the door as possible and getting excited about a walk after work because you can't get enough of this newfound energy.

Blah to Bling example: Before Mary knew it, the month had passed, and it was time for her visit to the doctor. She was very nervous. What the doctor told Mary was even more shocking than before: she had dropped her blood sugar in half and lowered her cholesterol by 100 points and her blood pressure was within normal levels—and on top of that, she had lost twelve pounds. She was amazed that changing her eating habits could make such a difference in one month. Although she had a way to go yet, her doctor was so pleased that she agreed to give her another month before starting the medications.

Mary raced out to tell her friend and get instructions on what to do next. She was told to continue with the healthy eating habits she had adopted but to be sure to mix up her choices, so boredom wouldn't set in. Her friend urged her to continue to read healthy magazines and books for ideas and inspiration.

The next habit was to add some movement, so she started walking just five minutes several times a day until she was walking fifteen minutes twice a day and building upon that habit.

When Mary returned to her doctor, she had dropped all her numbers down into a healthy range and was told she didn't need any medications. She was so excited that she had finally accomplished something she had struggled with all her life. She realized all it took was a plan, making small changes daily, and developing new habits to create huge results.

Add the Bling action step: Commit to at least fifteen minutes of activity. Build upon that until you reach thirty minutes five days a week. Choose things you enjoy and switch it up—variety is the spice of life.

Bling is choosing to exercise even when you don't want to because you know the benefits.

Blah is making excuses to skip the vital key to health, exercise.

Self-Discipline

"Discipline gives you the freedom to put all your energy into creating something meaningful and beautiful."

Self-discipline is a trait and a habit, one that is very important, and you should strive to develop because it determines the success of all the other habits. It is the bridge between thought and achievement. It's the secret key that unlocks doors; it alters the direction of your life. It overcomes procrastination and avoids the trap of instant pleasure which leads to settling. Never underestimate the power of self-discipline.

Force is a constraint exerted upon or against a person or thing. Power is possession of control, authority, or influence.

Perceiving discipline as a necessary part of getting what you want instead of viewing it as torture gives you the power to endure. Think of it as making one choice over another instead of something you are forced to do or a punishment. Eat this not that, think for yourself or allow others to do it for you, move or remain still, grown and learn or wither and regress. Discipline is nothing more than a series of choices that determine your results; it is the ability to think about what you want and then make the choices that will lead you in that direction.

Look at it as "I get to do this," not "I have to do this." Many of the things you view as having to do are things others would be grateful to be able to do, such as exercise. Those with disabilities would be thrilled to take a walk, go for a swim, or cut the grass. Self-discipline conquers the nagging voices of fear, failure, doubt, and procrastination.

Blah to Bling example: You decide you are going to implement the strategies outlined in this book, so you block out time for the development of the habits, traits, and mindsets. Your friend calls and wants you to go have drinks and dinner, and you had an early meeting that day, so you moved your self-development time block to evening. You want to join her, however that would mean giving up this important action you have decided will lead you toward changes you wish to see in your life. Also, if you go out you will probably be tired in the morning and sleep in which means missing tomorrow's action steps also. You decide that missing important disciplines you have selected to improve your results can easily lead to more missed actions needed to create the life you desire, so you choose to stay home. By building the habit of discipline you can move forward with developing other important habits.

Add the Bling action step: When you are faced with something you may not want to do, ask yourself what the rewards of doing this are. Focus on that answer because that will empower you. Remind yourself that you are not being forced to do the thing that needs to be done, you choose to.

Bling is creating disciplines that help you keep your promises to yourself so that you can create the life you choose.

Blah is allowing yourself off the hook every time you don't want to do something you know you should.

Program Your Mind

"Whatever you think about all the time is what you will attract to your life. Not what you want—what you think about."

To be your best, gain your confidence, and truly become who you wish to be, you must program your mind for those things. As I mentioned, confidence is not something you are just born with, no effort required. The most successful, confident people in the world constantly work to develop their confidence by conditioning their minds for success. You can only be your best, add the Bling to life, and maintain your results by believing in yourself, and that is accomplished through confidence.

The world today is it is just too noisy. You can't even hear yourself think—or should I say you don't really think because there is so much outside noise.

The problem with this is our subconscious, like a child, hears everything, especially what we don't want it to hear. Without you even knowing it, messages, thoughts, and ideas are being implanted all the time; that is why it's so important for you to choose your programing. Your mind, like your body, is what you feed it. If you fill it full of doubts, fears, and worries, that is what it will focus on. To have confidence, self-esteem, and self-worth, you must take time daily to infuse your thoughts with great things. You must take time to read encouraging, motivating, and inspiring things so you can view the world from the right perspective. You are faced daily with a barrage of negativity, falsehoods, and others trying to force their opinions on you. It is your job to shape the way you view the world and that can only be done by programing your mind.

If you find yourself in a position where the conversation is about things you don't want in your life, such as the government being corrupt, how the middle class can't get ahead, people just pushing through to retirement, people who hate their lives, people who say, "You only live once, so I will eat what I want, who cares?" or "My health issues are in my genes, there's nothing I can do about it," walk away now. The more you listen to these beliefs of others, the closer you become to making them yours.

This habit is the second most important thing you can do for yourself. (Health is number one.) Creating the atmosphere you wish to surround you is the difference between success and failure in all you do. It's hard sometimes to believe in yourself, to have courage, to push through limiting beliefs and to have confidence, but that is why you absolutely cannot skip this habit.

You need to build the habit of listening to motivating books, podcasts, and programs, as they will help condition your mind. Reading and journaling gets your creative thoughts flowing. Write down your goals and read them several times a day. Collect inspirational quotes that will stick in your head and keeping you thinking in the direction you wish to go. Exceptional people use some, if not all, of these methods to program their minds to make them the best that they can be. It is like building a shield around your thoughts to protect you from negative outside forces. Believe it or not, your thoughts are your reality; whatever you think about a thing makes it so. At the same time, others may think the total opposite: in their minds, that is true to them but not to you. What you are, will become, will achieve, and will have is all rooted in your thoughts. It is your job to program the thoughts you need to achieve your goals.

Blah to Bling example: How many people do you know who must have the TV on while they work? Not even to watch it, they just need noise. There is a commercial where a couple is camping, and they can't sleep. She says to him, "Listen to how quiet it is." He replies, "Yes," with a dissatisfied look. She says, "Is it too quiet?" He immediately replies, "Yes," grabs his phone, and turns on sounds of the city: horns blowing, sirens, and traffic. They fall fast asleep. This of course is a commercial for a phone app, but there is so much to be learned by it. We have become so hypnotized by outside forces that we can't even hear our thoughts any longer.

Add the Bling action step: Set aside at least 10 minutes a day to read or listen to something that will program your mind to think positively, that will provoke you to think and build belief in yourself.

Bling is taking time every day, as often as needed, to program your thoughts to the achievements you wish for.

Blah is not dedicating the time and effort needed to shape your mind, allowing it to be shaped by outside forces.

Personal Growth

"Nothing stands still—it is either growing or dying. There is nothing else."

Y ou must decide to never stop learning. Just because you've finished high school, college, or whatever it may be does not mean you are done. You must strive to learn, grow, and improve yourself and your knowledge every day. This doesn't mean you have to sign up for college courses or take on huge projects all the time. You just need to study yourself, look at life with an open mind, and always be willing to view things from a new perspective.

A weakness only remains if you ignore it and never try to improve it—any improvement, no matter how small, will help. You may not become an expert or the best at it, but you must attempt to learn more. No matter how strong, knowledgeable, or good at something you are, you must always be looking for ways to improve on your strengths as well. Your confidence is stronger than ever when you admit you have much to learn and look to others for their guidance. Acting as if you know it all and refusing to seek help will keep you from being your best. The whole purpose of existence is growth.

Maybe, for example, you would like to a better cook, even if that means simply being able to boil water. All you need to do is get some cookbooks, ask you mother, grandmother, or friends, or visit some websites to learn how. Any time you learn to be a little better than you are now, that is personal growth.

In youth we learn, in age we understand.

Select one of the mindsets, habits, or traits in this book and begin the journey to develop it, working through them one at a time. You may feel you have some under control, so you may want to start with the ones you feel you need most. Or maybe you want to work on ones that may seem a little easier to start so you can build your momentum. There is only one way to do it wrong and that is to not start today.

No one has all the traits, habits, or mindsets. Some have more than others, but the difference is that those who have the most or strongest habits are the ones who dedicate time toward their achievement. Even if you only develop one or two of them, you will see an increase in your confidence and your Bling. What is most important is constant, continuous growth—be careful not to allow yourself to slip into that mindset of perfectionism that says you must conquer all them before you can become Exceptional. Working toward developing yourself every day is far beyond ordinary. Every effort is an achievement.

Blah to Bling example: One day I was at my boat at the docks, and the girl next door and I were discussing books we had read and giving each other recommendations. Her dad, in his early 60s, overheard our conversation. He said, "I haven't read a book since I was in school," and he actually seemed proud of that fact.

His daughter, who seemed a bit embarrassed, replied, "Dad, I don't think I would brag about that." Although he seemed like a nice man, you could tell he had very low self-esteem and he never really believed he could be more based on how he compared his belongings to other more expensive ones all around. Along came some of his friends who jumped into the conversation, saying they didn't have time for reading either, that was for smart people. This hit me—even they viewed people who read as above them, more successful, but yet were not willing to put the effort forth to gain what they had. They had simply settled for being average, and it appeared that they supported each other's thoughts and beliefs on the subject.

Add the Bling action step: Starting today, decide you will learn one new thing every day. One small idea, thought, or insight is all you need.

Bling is making time to learn, grow, and develop yourself daily. It's not allowing any excuses because you know growth is vital to your confidence.

Blah is making excuses for why you can't make the time to do the things you need to grow, settling for less because you refuse to be more.

Think for Yourself

"Every day when you awake, open your eyes and say, 'I, not events or circumstances, have the power to make me who I choose to be.'"

Others push their beliefs on you every day, sometimes intentionally, but most of the time without any knowledge they are doing it. Most ideas, opinions, and beliefs are only imaginary formations with no basis; they trickle in so slowly they go unnoticed. Before you know it, you have a belief about something and have no idea why or any reasoning to back it. Confidence comes from not listening to the lies we all hear daily, not accepting a belief unless there is substance to it that it is based on facts, and most important of all, it agrees with your values.

It's all a matter of perception.

The most dangerous evil you can listen to is your own lies, the ones you tell yourself to justify something you did or said. You repeat them enough times that you really believe them and there is actually no truth to them at all.

Did someone say you are not smart enough to get a better job, or you are not good looking enough to attract a mate? Do you now tell yourself the same lies? Do you fool yourself into believing the reason you are not as successful as you would like is because you didn't get a fair chance?

Do you allow what others say to swirl around in your head until you believe it?

Thinking for yourself is about making choices based on your beliefs. Someone else's opinion does not determine who you are, who you can be, or what you can do, so don't allow yourself to think they do. Don't be afraid to be unique or speak your mind, because that's what makes you different from everyone else. Thinking for yourself requires you to step away from the tribe, to make a path where there may not be one. That is OK—it is your path. Don't let anyone else determine it for you.

Blah to Bling example: Suzi had a strong opinion about the controversial upcoming presidential election. She listened to others' opinions at work, watched the news, and kept up with it on social media. The issue was too much input from outside sources and not enough critical thinking on the inside. This led her to accept others opinions as her own, and before she knew what happened, she was following along with everything she heard without even considering any facts. She became a chameleon: whatever others said, she went along with.

The real issue once she developed this trait was that she started to accept whatever others said about everything. When others told her she couldn't do something, she accepted it as truth. It was a virus that spread to her own thinking; she would tell herself she wasn't good enough, or her opinion didn't matter anyway, so why say anything? She became a mere echo of what others thought because she gave up her right to think.

When she finally realized that she had become a ship without a rudder, bouncing from one person's opinion to another's, she decided it was time to speak up for herself. From that day forward, she walked away from the crowd and all the noise of the outside world and began to analyze her thoughts. When she didn't agree with others' opinions or outside sources, she did not argue; she simply made her decisions based on her own opinions after careful analysis.

Add the Bling action step: When you are forming an opinion, analyze the inputs around your thoughts. If you find yourself making decisions based on others' opinions, stop and think for yourself. Don't allow yourself to be swayed by mere perceptions or possible lies.

Bling is making your own choices, having your own perspectives and thoughts, and not going along with others blindly.

Blah is accepting what others say without questioning the facts or determining if it fits into your beliefs, making their opinions yours.

Make Decisions

"Indifference is a disease."

The cure for procrastination is action.

Decision is your ability to take action without questioning yourself. Decision trumps procrastination which will steal your dreams if not conquered. Life's journey is full of choices—make a decision and move forward, because when you fail to choose, you lock up your dreams. Never make decisions in haste just to make them, but don't paralyze yourself with indecision either. Not making a decision is a decision in itself: to sit back and let fate play its hand out and never influence it is not the way you were meant to live. You gain confidence when you decide for yourself because if you don't, someone else will do it for you, and they usually don't have your best interest in mind. Decision brings rewards; contemplation leads to missed opportunities.

Did you ever find yourself trying to decide where to go eat? You think, "I could go there, but maybe I should go here. What if I don't like the menu, or what if the service is bad, or my friends don't like it?" It's like a ping pong game in your head that becomes so distracting that you just decide to stay home.

Blah to Bling example: Carrie hated to make decisions, so she usually did what her best friend decided. Carrie's friend told her where they were going and when, what clothes to buy, and what to eat. It wasn't all her friend's doing; it just became the way things went. When faced with a decision, Carrie would simply not make up her mind. She feared the decision she made would be wrong, so instead thought she was playing it safe by not deciding and simply allowing things to happen in her life.

One day she looked around her life and thought to herself, "I really don't like most things I have, including my job. How did this happen? I didn't make any of these choices." By not taking action or making a decision, she had allowed everyone else to decide her destiny and she eventually found their idea of success looked quite different from hers. She realized by being so afraid to fail she did just that—she allowed her fear to keep her from making decisions that would create her life.

Add the Bling action step: Ask yourself, "What decisions have I been avoiding? What is this costing me?"

Bling is making a decision and following through, whether you want to or not; at least you have made that decision.

Blah is putting off making decisions, which delays action, refusing to keep your commitments to yourself.

Have a Purpose

"Purpose and meaning are created, not discovered."

B lah is blundering through life searching for your purpose and never getting anywhere because you feel you just haven't found it yet. Instead, create your purpose as you move forward, never wasting time on a fruitless search for meaning in your life.

 Confidence is knowing your purpose is to be you and believing that your gifts and talents will reveal themselves as you act on designing your life. Your purpose will be discovered one day at a time, so get out there and make it happen—don't hide behind the excuse of not knowing what your purpose is.

Success doesn't just find you. You must go out and get it.

If you want to know who you are, don't ask, act! Action will define you. Your future is of your own making. Your purpose in life is an ever-evolving quest: it can change, grow, and become crystal clear, but only if you act. Purpose gives you power and an obsession with moving forward; it keeps you from distractions and pulls you through difficulties. Don't wait for extraordinary opportunities; seize ordinary occasions and make them great.

Your purpose can be as simple as teaching a Sunday school class, performing in a play, or adopting a child, or as great as becoming a doctor or a scientist. Your purpose is a gift you have been given to share with the world and it changes all the time so don't make it more than it is and miss it all together by discounting your purpose.

Blah to Bling example: I spent a large portion of my life looking for my purpose. I would think I knew what it was and go in that direction, but when things didn't go well, I would decide that wasn't it after all and go back to the drawing board. I read numerous books and took several tests to find my weaknesses and strengths to try to guide me to my purpose. I spent countless hours in contemplation questioning just what it was I was supposed to do with my life. No matter how hard I tried, it just didn't seem to come to me, so I continued delaying taking action because I was afraid that if I started the wrong thing, I would miss my true purpose.

Then I read an eye-opening statement. It said, "Don't waste your life searching for meaning, get out there and create your purpose." I thought, "How can it be that simple? There is something inside I must discover." I was right, but the only way I was going to discover it was to start digging instead of searching.

The treasures were inside, but I was looking to outside sources to find them. As soon as I decided to just be me, my purpose and meaning in life revealed themselves. I hated to see others in despair, lonely, with no passion, helpless with no hope of a better tomorrow. My purpose is to give others hope, to help them find their passions and realize they never have to settle for what their current circumstance are and that they can be all they want to be. I just need to provide the tools to help them realize how to get from where they are to where they want to be, because I truly believe we all deserve the best life has to offer.

Add the Bling action step: Decide today to bring opportunity to you. Have a purpose and allow it to change as you do. Don't deliberate on your purpose, waiting for it to knock on your door.

Bling is creating Exceptional opportunities and developing your purpose with each one.

Blah is waiting for opportunity to find you—it won't unless you prepare for it.

Prioritize

"Don't serve time, make time serve you."

You cannot to do everything, be everything, or please everyone. Prioritizing is deciding what is important to you and making the things you have identified your focus. Once you do that, you then set goals in those areas and work on being your best. Remember, you want to hit your targets like a sharpshooter, not like a shotgun.

Prioritizing is simply identifying the most import things to you at the time, scheduling time for them, and filling in with the less important things. The rule is important things first.

Blah to Bling example. I was enjoying lunch with a dear friend. She had a good job, a nice home, a loving husband, two healthy, happy children, enjoyed a very modest lifestyle, went on vacations, drove a nice car, and was all and all very happy.

Out of the corner of my eye, I spotted another friend leaving the restaurant. I jumped to my feet to greet her and introduced my two friends. She sat down for just a moment because she said she was in a rush to catch a flight for an out-of-town meeting. I asked how she was doing and she told us she was doing extremely well: she just got a new Mercedes with all the bells and whistles, she had moved to a very high-end neighborhood this year and was looking at a second home in the Caribbean, she was wearing very expensive clothing and had a to-die-for leather bag and shoes. I ask how her family was, and she laughed as she said, "Good, when I get to see them." But she assured us they were well cared for by the housekeeper, nanny, and full-time staff she had. She then said her goodbyes and rushed out to jet around the world.

My friend looked at me and said, "Can you imagine living a life like that?"

I said, "I know, to have all those luxuries."

She shook her head and said, "No. I mean to have a life with no balance or fulfillment. She has money but no time to enjoy it or to spend with her family. What's the point?"

The point is you must look around your life and decide what is important and then make it a priority.

If your family is important, and I hope they are, schedule time around them, don't schedule them around other things of less importance. It is easy to do, life is busy, but being Exceptional means giving your best to what is most important.

If buying a new home or car is a top priority, you will need to plan your spending around saving for them.

If starting a new career or business or going back to school is what you have decided is important, you will need to schedule your activities around them, not the other way around.

If you must sacrifice your health, family, or peace of mind to have more luxuries, then they are not truly luxuries. They have control over you and will cause you to settle. This does not mean you should not want and work to have nice things; it simply means the greatest luxury is balance in all that you do.

Add the Bling action step: At the end of the day reflect back on what you did that day. Ask yourself, "Did I keep my priorities in line?" If the answer is no, plan tomorrow allowing for them first.

Bling is doing the things that are important to you first, not allowing others' agendas or distractions to keep you from yours.

Blah is determining that being home for dinner with your family is a priority and then allowing a project at work to make you miss it.

Section 4:
Struggles

Don't Wish It Was Easier, Strive to Be Better

Life is full of struggles; just because you are confident does not mean you will not have battles to fight. The difference between conquering them and letting them conquer you is knowing we are all human and most of us struggle with many of the same issues. Seeking guidance with your struggles helps you realize you are not alone which gives you courage.

The first step in overcoming your struggles is identifying them. You can't work on correcting something you cannot see. The best way to move forward is to bring your struggles to the surface, deal with them, learn to manage them, and move past them.

You will struggle with adjusting your mindset to think in different ways, but you must fight the thought that you cannot develop the traits or build the habits to become confident. You will certainly think the action steps and strategies are too much work or uncomfortable, and you are not alone. However, if you want to become confident, Exceptional, and someone you are not, you will have to struggle your way through.

Accepting Yourself

"The person that can free themselves from self-imposed beliefs that are not true will gain acceptance."

The worst loneliness is to be uncomfortable with yourself.

Accepting yourself as you are is a challenge. You never think you are good enough or measure up to others. This is a struggle suffered by everyone, so you are not alone by any stretch of the imagination. You should never settle for mediocre and you should always be striving to improve yourself; however, the key to advancement is appreciating where you are now. If you don't like who you are, your internal voices will destroy your chances of escape. It's OK to not like your current circumstances; those will change as soon as you decide they will. The realization you must have is that person you don't like comes along to the new circumstances too. Although some things may have changed, if you don't make peace with yourself, you are dragging along that enemy within.

Are you your own worst enemy? Do you look in the mirror and think, "I have a strange nose," "I have terrible hair," or "I'm fat"? Do you stand in the line at the grocery store and think, "She is so much more attractive than me"? Or when at the office, do you overhear someone getting praise for a job well done and think, "I could never have done that"?

Acceptance is the first step to change.

You are a wonderful human being with genius inside, talents, skills, gifts to share, and a purpose to serve, and you deserve the very best life has to offer. Maybe you got off track or off to the wrong start, but your circumstances do not determine you, you do—and just because you may have made some bad choices does not change the fact that you are a great person. Every day you have the opportunity of a fresh start.

Before someone told us we couldn't do something, we just did it.

Your beliefs can hold you back, limit your growth, and control you unless you learn to push past them, paying them no attention. Don't let old patterns, habits, or self-limiting beliefs keep you from your dreams. Develop competence: it is your confidence to push beyond your limiting beliefs. You need practical skills. You cannot artificially inflate your self-esteem; it requires victories, accomplishments, and constantly conditioning your mind. Beliefs come from experience, so stay enthusiastic even through setbacks, know you can do it, and step into it. Be maniacal in your beliefs and determination—this will allow you to truly believe in yourself.

Blah to Bling example: Tina was never happy. She always told herself, "I will be happy when I get a better job, make more money, and get in better shape."

Well, all of those things happened, and she still wasn't happy, so she convinced herself she needed other things to become happy. She bought new clothes, remodeled her house, got a new car, and got a makeover, but still she was not happy.

It was only after a deep evaluation of her feelings that she realized the problem: it wasn't the image in the mirror, it was that evil voice inside. No matter what she did, she couldn't outrun it. Even though she changed her circumstances, she still couldn't escape the wrath of that voice. It was when she realized she had to make friends with the voice within that she finally found happiness. Understanding she could only be her best once she learned to accept herself as she was now was the key to improvement. She finally quit trying to run from herself.

Add the Bling action step: When someone complements you, say "Thank you" without following it with a degrading comment. Graciously accepting compliments does not make you arrogant; they felt you deserved it, and so should you.

Bling is learning to be your own best friend, loving who you are but not being ego-driven.

Blah is degrading yourself, finding fault in all you do and who you are.

Belittling Yourself

"There is no contest to be you."

Comparing yourself to anyone else but your best self is belittling and destroys you. If your significant other takes notice of someone attractive, that does not mean you are not equally attractive and desirable, it simply means they are human just like you. We all like to look at the scenery sometimes, but that doesn't mean we want to change our current view.

Never judge a book by its cover; realize what is going on inside can be very different than the front others are putting on. It may be a disguise to protect their feelings, insecurities, or fears. Acknowledge that we all have our own little battle going on inside and strive to gain the skills and tools to overcome it. Always act in accordance with your goals; do not give in to your internal battle. You have heard the advice "Fake it till you make it"—well, that is good advice because the more you portray confidence, the easier it gets to truly be confident.

Affirm yourself, don't degrade yourself.

Do not berate yourself when you are faced with others who appear to have it all together, to be successful, confident, and attractive. Instead try to learn from them, understand what makes them appear that way and how you can do it too. Even the most confident deal with feelings of fear, doubt, insecurity, and failure.

Have you ever prepared for a big promotion? You got a haircut, bought a new suit, polished your shoes, and prepared your presentation. You were ready to take the world by storm, you walked into the waiting room on fire. Once inside, you looked around and soon started judging how everybody looked compared to you. You glanced over your shoulder to see one of the other fellows working on his 3D presentation which you feel is superior to yours. The next thing you know, you feel like a mouse in the corner, cowering and beaten. All the wind is knocked out of your sails and you just want to leave.

Blah to Bling example: "Keeping up with the Joneses" is the reason so many suffer through life. I watched a Christmas movie about several families that were always trying to outdo one another. One family had decorated their home beautifully, but when they saw the neighbors' decorations, they ran out to buy more. So then the other neighbors did the same thing, and it went on and on. That led to competing for the best holiday party, each planning a more elaborate event than the other. Next came the contest to buy the best gifts, each spending way more than they could afford which caused fighting and stress.

Across the street was another family who watched in amusement as their neighbors battled to outdo one another. They however did not get caught up in the game; they decorated, shopped, and planned their modest holiday party. The neighbors all sneered and talked behind their backs about how pitiful they were. They invited everyone on the block to their holiday get-together, and reluctantly they all went because they were afraid the others might go, and they would be the only ones left out.

It was a beautiful party. It wasn't fancy, but what they found was that these people were happy and were truly enjoying the holiday. With embarrassment they looked at each other and realized they had destroyed their entire season because they got so caught up in comparing themselves to each other. They stole their own joy from themselves by berating their own efforts, comparing themselves to others, and never just accepting what they had was fine the way it was. They allowed insecurity to control them.

Add the Bling action step: The next time you feel inferior to someone, don't judge yourself against them—instead ask yourself, "What do they have that I wish to have?" Ask them how they achieved the success you desire instead of beating yourself up; it's counterproductive. Get to work getting it for yourself. They had to work for it too.

Bling is having the confidence to appreciate the beauty in others without comparing yourself to them. They are probably fighting the same battle inside looking at you.

Blah is accepting defeat when you are faced with others who are or have what you want.

Mind Mastery

"Rule your emotions, don't let them rule you."

Master your mind or it will master you.

When you have negative thoughts, they rule you. You are always looking for ways to make them happy, but that will never happen because they are in control; they will always want more until they have consumed you and taken over. Positive thoughts work in the same way so you must choose your dictator wisely.

Confidence comes from mastering your mind, thoughts, and emotions and learning how to throw the switch to empowering thoughts. Become the mind master; arm yourself with ways to quickly take charge when the enemies try to invade and turn you into a slave. Eliminate over-analysis and second guessing. Focus your attention only on what you want with great positivity.

Just because you have feelings of guilt doesn't actually make you responsible. Not everything is your fault; you can't do it all or be it all and you certainly cannot please everyone. Others will try to control you through your guilt: if their event is a flop, they don't get what they want, or things didn't turn out as they planned, they may try to use the emotional card to evoke blame.

Bling is not accepting fault for others' wishes that are not your wishes. Make the choices that are in line with your agenda, accept the consequences for your choices and actions. It is not your fault if things don't work out for others exactly as they had hoped although they may try to pin it on you. Fault is when you deliberately do something to harm another; choosing what is best for you does not make it wrong, even if others feel it is.

Did you ever turn down a friend because you just had too many things going on in your life at that time? They became offended and made some kind of a comment to others that they really needed your help and it is your fault if they fail. Did you allow that to eat away at you, questioning yourself, wondering "Should I have tried to squeeze that in?"

If you want something, don't let your inner dialog talk you out of it.

In his article published in 1990, Dr. R. J. Korba, Department of Communication, College of Wooster, reported that the human brain says more than 4,000 words per minute to itself—that is a lot of noise going on in there! Just imagine how that affects you. Your internal dialog can either make or break you.

Confidence is choosing the words you allow to enter your thoughts, starting with your own words to yourself. You carry your words with you everywhere, all day long. If the words you say to yourself are demeaning, destructive, or self-defeating, how can you be confident?

Many times, the words going on in your head were put there by others. Choose wisely what you allow yourself to hear from others and, more importantly, from yourself—if it is not what you should hear to be confident, don't listen.

The only limit to your capabilities is the one you place on yourself.

Whatever your dreams, goals, or desires are, you are the only one keeping you from them. Looking in the mirror and owning that fact is key to your confidence. It will be a battle of You versus You until you accept this reality and push your fearful, doubting self aside. You must stop underestimating yourself and taking yourself for granted. Stop dwelling on failures, mistakes, and imperfections, and instead appreciate your achievements. Put on your big girl (or boy) pants and decide to gain the skills and knowledge you need to accomplish your goals. Go do it! No excuses.

Blah to Bling example: Emily went to college and graduated top of her class. She was a highly educated, knowledgeable, beautiful woman. The only one who didn't know this was her. She always told herself, "You're not smart enough. You're not as pretty as the other girls. Why would anyone want to be your friend, marry you, or hire you?"

Others could sense her low confidence and took advantage. They made her the scapegoat instead of taking blame for their own actions. They learned to control her by manipulating her emotions, making her feel guilty if she didn't do what they wanted. The feelings of guilt evoked doubt, worry, anger, shame, and just about every other negative feeling. Her emotions were a runaway train leading down the track of indecision, despair, and procrastination, literally ruining her life.

One day, after spending her entire day as bundle of nerves, she said to herself, "Enough is enough. My life is completely out of control." She began to reprogram her mind through the help of a coach, listening to empowering messages, reading books full of inspiring messages, and journaling to get the negative emotions out of her head. Emily is now much more confident and happy, and she is pursuing her dreams. She has made programing her mind a daily habit because she realizes that emotions will control her life unless she controls them. She has vowed to never let others manipulate her through her emotions, especially not herself.

Add the Bling action step: Before you act or make a decision, ask yourself, "Is this what I really want or are my emotions out of control?" Remind yourself emotions are not reasonable; they are greedy, self-centered control freaks.

Bling is not allowing your emotions to run your life or control your actions.

Blah is allowing your inner dialog to talk you out of something you want.

Perfectionism

"There is no confidence in perfect."

If you are struggling with self-confidence, it is almost certain that you suffer from perfectionism. Although it is probably the furthest thing from your mind because you believe you are not even close to perfect, that is perfectionism. You are right, you're not perfect—I'm not perfect, nobody is perfect, so get over it because until you do you can never have confidence. We set standards for ourselves that can never be met. We are flawed. We make mistakes and have fears and doubts but that is OK. We are all in the same boat together; we all share in this fear of not being enough that keeps us stuck.

Keep in mind you cannot be all things to all people, not everyone will like you, you can't do it all, and there are things some are just going to do better. You are only human, just like everyone else. So discover who you are and be you! Do not compare yourself to or compete with others; instead focus on your strengths and accept your limitations. There is no contest to be you. You will have to learn to accept your uniqueness and give yourself the respect you are due. You are a wonderful, unique, once-in-all-history event, but you are not perfect. Life's challenges are to be cherished as a gift to help you grow, not just a problem to overcome.

If you put off everything until you are sure of it, you will never do anything.

Perfect does not exist and the sooner you realize this, the more confident you will be. Thinking you must be perfect pushes you even further away from the very thing you are striving for because it creates insecurity, doubt, and procrastination, which totally paralyzes you and leads to certain failure. Accept that striving for perfection is an unachievable dream.

Did you have a great idea that you wanted to share with the world but kept it inside because is just wasn't quite good enough yet? Have you written poetry that is tucked away until the day you think it is just right? Do you have a dream inside you that you are afraid to live until it is perfect?

Bling is doing your best and working toward improving who you are but at the end of the day accepting you are not perfect. Perfect is the enemy of great. When you chase perfection, you have a lot of projects still in the "development" queue, and this includes developing you—all these projects never get started because you are continually refining them. The fact is, however, most flaws that you see are not flaws others will see. Let go of the hesitation because you are searching for perfect and just do it. Great and done is better than perfect but never started.

Blah to Bling example: I am the walking, breathing example of a perfectionist. Everyone who knows me will confirm it and it has plagued my life because its twin sister is procrastination, the number one destroyer of all success. I have spent my life dreaming of a career where I help others believe in themselves, guide them to become their best, and share my knowledge to inspire, empower, and provoke happiness. However, I did not fulfill that dream until after my 50th birthday.

In one of the hundreds of classes I took looking for the one lesson that would finally vindicate me as good enough to try, the teacher said, "Go to your journals to discover yourself." The class was on writing and his thought was that most writers keep journals and that is where you will find pure gold because we have patterns that appear over and over. So, I took that tip and went back to my first journal and started to read. What I discovered was a true awakening: there in my own words were my dreams splattered all over, page after page, year after year. So why then had I not taken action?

That answer was there as well: I wasn't good enough yet, I needed a little more training, if I started too soon I might fail, others won't listen to me. I just wasn't perfect yet. This, of course, led to procrastination. I was living a life of tomorrows and I realized that until I gave up on being perfect, I was never going to be happy. I had to accept that life is not always going to go as planned and circumstances will lead me down paths I didn't expect. But the point is I had to get on my journey, I couldn't just sit on the sidelines wondering what direction to take. Life could only show me the way if I was on the path. I needed to shake off the "what if's. My horizon became clearer as

I began moving forward—right or wrong, I was at least taking action.

Add the Bling action step: Google perfectionism and read several of the definitions. Do they hit home? Are they describing you? For me the answer was a resounding YES, however I didn't realize that was my struggle. I just kept telling myself "I'm not ready yet." It is only when I realized that in my mind I was never going to be good enough that I was able to move forward. I delayed writing this book because I didn't think it was good enough. Once I faced my greatest struggle, I realized I had great things to say and others needed to hear them.

Bling is knowing in your heart it may not be perfect, but it is your best possible now. Do it and improve on it as you go.

Blah is putting off things because they are not yet perfect, always procrastinating till tomorrow.

Procrastination

"Sometimes later becomes never. Do it now."

Procrastination = Mediocrity.

Failure and defeat are the result of procrastination. Perfectionism, accepting mediocrity, and settling are contributing factors to it. If you are always putting things off till tomorrow, you live in never-never land. The cure is action. You must develop the ability to act when you don't want to, are afraid to, or doubt you can do it.

Procrastination is when you say, "I will call my mother tomorrow," or "I will get a checkup after I lose a few pounds." It is telling yourself you will go back to school when you make more money or you will play with the kids as soon as you finish this report. Procrastination is delaying living your life right now.

Procrastination is another word for excuse. You can only achieve your hopes, dreams, and goals if you decide to do it and then move forward now—not in a minute or after you finish this or that, *now*. It hides behind many faces: when you busy yourself with other tasks that have nothing to do with your goals, this is a form of procrastination, even if you are telling yourself this must be done. Prioritize your goals and get to work. If what you are doing doesn't lead you toward those goals, stop right now—you are procrastinating.

Blah to Bling example: Gloria always put everything off: She was going to exercise when she retired. She would take a vacation next year when she had more money. She was going to go back to school for that degree she had always wanted. She would take time to visit family and friends next weekend, she would have a checkup next month. Everything in her life was always at a time in the future; she never took any action today for one reason or another.

On her way to work one day, she got a sharp pain and tightening in her chest. She quickly pulled to the side of the road. She thought, "This can't be a heart attack, I can't die, I haven't done all the things I want to do yet." Her thoughts were racing fasting than her pulse— "This can't be, I haven't lived my life yet."

The next thing she remembered was the sounds of sirens and voices all around her in a panic saying, "We are losing her." "Who are they talking about? Where am I? What is going on?" She pleaded, "Please don't let me die, I still have so much to do. I promise I will start tomorrow."

Several days later, she awoke in the hospital with her family all around her. She asked, "Am I alive? Is this a dream?" When they convinced her she was still breathing, she decided it was time to live today, not tomorrow. She was grateful for another chance to take action, realizing that her life would only begin when procrastination stopped.

Add the Bling action step: Make a plan of action steps toward the accomplishment of your goals. Block out time to work on them and if you find yourself doing something else, realize procrastination has set in and get back to the task at hand.

Bling is setting a goal, designing the action steps to achieve it, and taking action now.

Blah is telling yourself you aren't quite ready and you will get started tomorrow.

Taking Time for Yourself

"Honor yourself: it is a necessity. It is not being selfish, it's caring for oneself."

You must set aside time for you. Take this very seriously and protect it with your life because others will always be trying to steal it. You lose yourself if you don't make time to do the things you love: relax, read a book, work out, go shopping, have a night out, whatever it is you enjoy doing, you must do it. Reality often swamps you and paralyzes your imagination. You need time to let your mind play, relax, and regenerate. Give yourself and your mind a treat; do something for you.

Allowing time for yourself is relaxing in a bubble bath after everyone is in bed—the emails will wait. Have a glass of wine while watching the flames in the fireplace dance, alone with your thoughts. Go shopping for something personal, not groceries or household needs. Have a cup of tea with your journal in the morning before the day starts. Taking time for yourself is a walk through the leaves on a cool crisp fall day with you best friend, two- or four-legged. Me time is nothing more than carving out a few precious moments here and there to care for you.

Me time is not selfish, it's necessary.

Blah To Bling

When you work all the time and give of yourself constantly, your efficiency will soon suffer. There is no faster way to burnout. Don't fall into the habit of denying yourself the time you need to recharge. You can't do it all, no matter how much you think you can. You really don't want to say yes but feel obligated to do so when asked because you don't want to let anyone down. The person you let down the most when you don't say no is yourself. Failure to say no and mean it—by that I mean not feeling guilty for saying no, not giving in later—will steal your Bling.

Blah to Bling example: Carol was a very busy lady and prided herself on how well she took care of everyone around her. She was like Superwoman: she worked a full-time job, did all the cooking, cleaning, and shopping, packed lunches, did laundry, ran errands, decorated her home for all occasions, and had holiday dinners for everyone. When asked to do a favor, volunteer, or just about anything else, she always said yes.

As time went on, Carol grew tired because she did so much without ever asking for any help. Others had come to assume she would just handle it. She began to lose who she was because she no longer did any of things she loved doing; there was no time. She was up early and went to bed late trying to get everything done. When the thought of sitting down with a cup of tea and enjoying a good book came up, she quickly told herself, "You can't do that, it would be selfish. There is so much to do."

Carol became ill, so she visited her doctor. He told her she was stressed out and that was destroying her health. He prescribed some downtime immediately: she needed to relax, or she was going to suffer greater consequences. She didn't have a clue how to do that, so she visited the counselor he recommended. There she was given guidelines on how to delegate some of the duties, how to say no to things she didn't really wish to do but felt obligated to, and how to deal with her guilt. It took time and required her to look at things in a different way but soon she was feeling better and was accomplishing far more of the things that were important to her instead of being bogged down with things that didn't bring her joy. She realized holding others accountable was not selfish or mean—it actually helped them become more independent—and that not everything was her responsibility.

Add the Bling action step: When faced with a request you really do not have time for, graciously thank them for thinking of you but firmly, without hesitation, say, "I'm sorry I have to decline. It sounds like a great opportunity, but I simply have a full schedule."

Bling is knowing you deserve time for you—it isn't a gift, it is your right.

Blah is always giving up your time which leads to resentment and lack of passion.

Section 5:
Strategies to Develop and Maintain Your Bling

In this chapter, you will learn the key strategies for developing your confidence, gain insights on how to maintain your level of confidence, and learn the tools you need to go from Blah to Bling.

The strategies are laid out in order, so you can begin with the most important one. I suggest you start with number one and work your way through in order because they build upon one another. If you have already conquered a strategy, move on to the next. It is very important to take each one very seriously and understand how they all work together to help you accomplish becoming your best and most confident self.

All suggested worksheets can be found at my website, FromBlahtoBling.com, for your convenience.

Strategy #1: Determine Your Goals

Purpose:

*Establish your starting point

*Design your road map for accomplishing your goals

*Identify your "Why"

*Create focus

When determining your goals, you need to set goals you really want to achieve for yourself, not for someone else; they need to be deeply rooted in your desires and emotions. Goals need to give you meaning and purpose. Forget about goals you chose because you felt pressured to select them, because you felt you "should"—these are not your goals, unless your goal is to live your life based on what others want from you. You must select goals you are passionate about; if you don't, you will be a pinball in the game of life and all outside sources will have control over you. Simply saying "I want confidence" is not a strong enough reason—you must have a burning desire with huge payoffs to keep you going. You must be clear on what you want and why you want it to actually achieve it.

Building confidence begins with achievement. When you have daily successes, this will move you closer to being confident. Having goals is the first step to gaining your confidence. You cannot go through life without goals if you wish to be confident or successful because you will not have a target to aim for.

Thoughts may be flashing through your head like: "I have no clue what I want, so how do I determine my goals?" Great, you have just established your first and most important goal: determining what you want.

Step 1: Brainstorm

Get out paper and a pen and write down everything you enjoy, like, or want. Don't rush this, just let your thoughts flow onto the paper and get down as many things as you can think of. Don't judge, just write. Then write down all the things you don't like, don't enjoy doing, or don't want in your life. Put them side by side and compare them: are there things on your like side that conflict with your dislikes? If so, that may not be a good goal. Keep in mind you may need to do things that you may not like in order to achieve your goals, however if the dislikes overshadow the likes, you probably won't accomplish that goal.

Example: My goal was to help others gain confidence, give them hope, and guide them to be their best. I thought the way to do this was to be a professional speaker, so I started on that journey. I soon realized all the things I needed to do to become successful had far more dislikes than likes. I had not taken time to understand the things I didn't like outweighed what I truly desired. I did not want to spend my life on the road and in airports alone. The dislikes were burying my likes until I could no longer see my goals, and I was going to give up on my dream. It was when I discovered the brainstorming exercise that I realized I needed to change how I would achieve my dream instead of giving up on it.

Step 2: Create a master goals list

List as many goals as you want on the master sheet, and add more as you get them.

Goals must be written down—this shows commitment and dedication. Without that, they are merely dreams.

Example: Some goals you might list are things like: learn new skills, get a new career, lose weight, take better care of yourself, get organized, write a book, start a business, buy a home, buy a car, go on a vacation, become a better person, eat more plant-based foods, quit smoking, spend more time with your family.

Step 3: Select 3 top goals

Review your master list and pick the three most important goals to you right now. Put them in order of importance.

Example: Your top three may be:

1) Take better care of yourself

2) Get more organized

3) Start a business

Step 4: Prepare goal sheets

Write each goal on the top of a goal sheet, one for each of the three goals, along with the numbered priority you have given it. Steps 5-8 will be recorded on these sheets.

Step 5: Write down the rewards of achieving each goal

You will need to create a clear mental imagine of what the goal will look like once you have achieved it. This step is the motivation for pursuing the goal. Having a clear mental image ignites your emotions of love, happiness, joy, fulfillment, purpose and meaning. These feelings alone are a huge reward.

Example: Your goal to take better care of yourself will give you energy and confidence because you will feel better. Your newfound energy will give you ambition to try new things, a whole new outlook on life. Achieving this goal will be the start of accomplishing your other goals.

Step 6: Write down the consequences of not achieving your goals

Visualizing what your life will look like without accomplishing your goals is also very motivating; it evokes emotions of anger, fear, doubt, and worry. As we have discussed, these emotions can keep us from our dreams, so use the power of them to inspire you instead.

Example: If you don't take better care of yourself, your health will suffer. You will struggle with illness and lack of energy and vibrancy. You won't feel like doing the things you need to achieve your goals, so you will remain stuck in your current circumstances. You will waste precious time on doctor visits or downtime due to illness. What confidence you do have will suffer because of your self-image—it is very hard to be confident when you don't feel or look good due to neglecting yourself. Everything in your life will suffer when you fail to take care of yourself.

Step 7: Write down the action steps you need to take

A goal without action is merely a dream, so write down the actions you will need to take to achieve the goal. Write as many as you can think of right now, and remember you can add, delete, or change them as you move toward your goal. Now determine the most important steps, the three to seven things you need to do today to get moving.

Example: Your goal to become more organized might look like this:

Purchase some books or programs on organizing my tasks

2)   Schedule time to read and learn about organization

3)   Choose a day planner

4)   Start small, schedule my day

Step 8: Write down the skills you will need to develop

You may not know which skills you will need, so start with researching others who have accomplished your goals. This will help you determine what skills you have that may need improvement or which skills you need to develop. Keep in mind you can develop any skill—successful people were not born with their skills; they created them, and you can too.

Example: If your goal is to start a business*:*

1)   Business planning

2)   Marketing

3)   Product knowledge

4)   People skills

5)   Accounting

Step 9: Revisit and rewrite goals weekly

Writing your goals over and over embeds them into your mind; it makes you focus on them. It strengthens your will and dedication to them, adds clarity, and allows you to adjust as you progress. The mere act of writing creates excitement and creativity. If you really want to accomplish your goals more quickly, write them daily.

Tools needed:

Journal, which you can download for free as a thank you gift. Simply log on to my website fromblahtobling.com

Binder, to assemble your journal pages in

Paper to fit the binder size you have selected

Strategy #2: Action Planning

Purpose:

*Get the most important tasks done first

*Allow you to move from task to task without guilt

*Give you more time for you

*Help balance your life and tasks

*Prevent overwhelm and burnout

Now that you have determined your goals and know your target, it is time to design your plan. Achievement does not come from winging it—although you do need to be able to think quickly on your feet, that alone will not get you to your goals. Planning your actions is the key ingredient to success; failing to do so will lead to shotgun effect results. You will graze many things but never really hit any targets, which leads to frustration, overwhelm, discouragement, and eventually failure.

Blocking out time to take action creates focus and eliminates distractions, allowing you to get things done in a timely manner. It forces you to actually sit down and pick the few things of most importance to get done today. Remember you can only do so much, so don't get carried away with the number of tasks for the day or you will become overwhelmed as well.

The key is to schedule the time as an appointment and treat it as such: tune out all distractions, including phones, kids, chores, and anything else that will take your mind off the task at hand (unless, of course, nature calls— you'd better answer that one or you really will be distracted!). Set a timer if you need to and work on that task for that allotted time period. When the time is up, put it aside and move on to the next task in your schedule. Giving your full attention to the project for that time frees your mind because it gives you a sense of accomplishment and that leads to growing confidence.

Scheduling your actions into smaller time frames helps you tackle large, overwhelming goals because it allows your brain to focus. Knowing you only must work on one thing for that time frees you of guilt and allows you to get other things done as well without the burden of thinking you should keep your nose to the grindstone until it is done. Sometimes we will have deadlines and those projects will require more time, so you'll need to schedule according to your priorities—however, do not push yourself beyond your limits or give up other things that need your attention. Life is about balance. Your goals should be aimed at the achievement of balance in your life, and time blocking will give you that. The key is to forget the task when the time is up and move on to whatever else you have planned without guilt or regret.

Example: I call this strategy "action planning" because action is what you need to plan, not time or tasks. I was a master at planning my tasks on my calendar, choosing different colors for each one and filling my day. On my calendar, I looked like the most productive person you have ever seen, but my problem was taking action on those tasks. I still lacked focus: an email, a phone call, or many other things would still distract me. I would tell myself, "Just this one call, text, or thing and I will get back on track." Wrong. Before I knew it, one thing led to another and I was completely off my schedule.

"No worries," I would think, "I'll simply rearrange the tasks to correct my schedule." The problem with that was I had already lost precious time and now I was wasting more juggling the tasks around. I either had to shorten the allotted time, push the task to tomorrow, or completely delete something, none of which were good options because it meant either rushing through the work, not being my best, or skipping things I had determined were important. This created brain overload, guilt, and Blah, because I was stealing my own Bling.

Planning is your road map to avoiding detours, setbacks, and bumps in the road. It helps you stay the course, so you arrive at your desired location. Without a plan, you tend to follow the tribe because you are lost, and the problem with that is that most of the time, where others are going is not where you want to go. By the time you realize they really don't have a good plan either—or have no plan at all—you are so lost you keep following them into the jungle.

Life is about balance, so you will need to schedule to dos, personal time, work, projects, time to program your mind, appointments, and whatever you need to do. The key is to not overwhelm yourself. Simply block three to five actions a day, based on your biggest goals, and forget the rest until those are complete.

Step 1: Select your planner

This is about what works for you. What's important is your planner is something you have access to always to keep you on track. I prefer Google Calendar because I can block my time in different colors to make it visually appealing and to track categories of projects.

Step 2: Select 3-5 actions for the day

Review your master list and select the most important things for that day. Remember to keep them attainable—you can only do so much in a day, and that is OK. Choose wisely.

Step 3: Designate how much time you will allow for each action

Large projects may need to be spread over days, weeks, months, or sometimes years. Your time blocks should be focused around the goals you have selected. The actions should be priorities, and should be scheduled first.

Step 4: Set reminders to keep you on track

Set timers to remind you when to start and stop your projects. Without this step, you can easily go over your allotted time. Set one for fifteen minutes before your time is up and another for when time is up to help you wrap up the current task for this time frame and move onto the next.

Tools needed:

A calendar to track your actions. It needs to be one you can keep with you always; I suggest one that can be used on many devices to make it easy to access anywhere. Choosing a calendar with built-in reminders helps keep things simple as well. I personally like Google Calendar because I can check it on my PC, tablet, or phone, it allows me to choose colors for each action which keeps them from running into one another at a glance, and it has built-in reminders. It also has task lists I can create. I have lists for today, this week, this month, and a master list. As things come to mind that I need or want to accomplish, I put them on the master list and then prioritize them in my action plan based on their importance, leading me toward my most important goals.

Strategy: #3 Journal

Purpose:

*Discover your true thoughts

*Reveal limiting beliefs, so you can replace them with empowering ones

*Uncover behavior patterns that are holding you back

*Learn from your history

Part of knowing where you are going is knowing where you are and where you came from. Your journal is a place to be you, discover who you are, and learn invaluable wisdom. It is a reference book for your thoughts, feelings, and knowledge. It is a chapter in your book of life.

Morning is a great time to capture your true feelings, to get whatever is bouncing around in your head onto paper. Maybe it's negative or doubtful thoughts, and getting them out first thing will allow you to move forward in a positive mood. Reflect on yesterday so you can learn from your successes and failures, which helps you know where to improve and what to build upon. Our minds are fresh in the morning which allows us to brainstorm ideas, thoughts, and insights.

Blah To Bling

Your journal is your place where you let it all come out. No one is going to read it but you, so don't be afraid to let your hair down, get it all out. Your journal will be a great resource to you in the future, so keep it handy for inspirations as they pop up, so you can capture them. You may prefer an electronic journal, so you don't have to carry it around; the choice is yours. The important thing is to have one, use it, and go back and read it. However, keep in mind that studies show the act of putting pen to paper brings about creative juices. Once you begin, the thoughts will flow.

You are probably thinking, "I don't have time for journaling," but the truth is you don't have time to *not* journal. It is one of the quickest ways to develop your road map to the life you want, so quit wasting time you don't have fussing about whether to write in your journal or not—do it.

You need to get the Blah, the negative, doubting troublemakers, out in the open so you don't have to carry them around with you all day, and bring the Bling to the forefront to motivate you and inspire you. By taking some quiet time with your thoughts, you will discover things you didn't even know about yourself. It will help you reveal ideas to improve your life you didn't even know you had.

Example: I use a method I discovered for overcoming a challenge. Every day, I would write about the issue I was having. Over and over, every day, I would write my thoughts and feelings around what I was struggling with.

The method is based on making realizations and breaking a cycle, so you can change it.

One of my greatest struggles was weight loss, so every morning I would write about my thoughts surrounding the subject. At first it sounded like a pity party but then it evolved into thoughts of "Why do I let this control me and upset me?" and "How do I change this?" Before I knew it, I was writing about ways to take better care of myself, reflecting on what I did well the day before and what I would do today. I wrote about my feelings around food, health, and weight, and changes I saw in my body and in my appearance, but mostly in my mindset.

What revealed itself to me was that I needed to stop the torture, the sacrifice, the crazy diets, and the mindset of dieting altogether. I realized I was on a treadmill going nowhere, always focusing on the end when I could get off, and as soon as I did, I was right back where I started. My journal gave me the answer to my life-long struggle and I put that all behind me and now live a very happy, healthy, fit lifestyle.

I am not a perfect size 5 or at a particular number on the scale, but I now focus on healthy eating. By allowing my thoughts to come out instead of suppressing them, I was able to confront them. I had been acting as if the issue didn't exist, that it didn't bother me. By going back over my thoughts, I realized my weight issues affected more than I acknowledged—obviously if I wrote about them every day. I will save those details for my upcoming book that tells you how to get off the weight loss roller coaster as well.

Step 1: Block 10-15 minutes for journaling at the start of your day

Get yourself a journal today and get writing. This may seem like a struggle to fit into your day, but once you get started, you will look forward to your time with your thoughts. Throughout history, the great people, women and men alike, have used journals to achieve success in all areas. Achievement is about habits you develop; once in place, they become like second nature to you—you don't think about them, you just do them. The key here is to get the thoughts out of your head and onto the paper, so you can dissect them for limiting beliefs, traits, patterns, dreams, goals, and inspiration.

Step 2: Begin with gratitude

Start your entry with at least one thing you are grateful for at that moment. Even more is better, but at least write one. This will get your thoughts flowing and set the pace.

Step 3: Read your journal

Your journal is not something you will write in and then put on a shelf; you must go back and read the thoughts, inspirations, insights, and emotions. You will discover pure gold within the pages; you will discover patterns, realize how much your perspective on things has changed, and reveal struggles you may not even realize you have.

Start with day one when you began to journal, working toward today. Read what you wrote (just one daily entry is enough), highlighting the limiting beliefs you discover and the thought patterns and the habits that are controlling or limiting you.

Tools needed:

A journal small enough to keep with you at all times

Your favorite comfortable pen

It is important that your journal suit your needs, that it feels comfortable, like your favorite pair of old jeans. You want your journal time to be like spending time with your best friend. It will become your security blanket that you enjoy turning to, not something you have to do.

Paper and pen are my choice because it helps my creative thoughts flow, while electronic devices tend to block them. This isn't just my belief, studies actually find this to be true. Whatever your choice, it doesn't matter—just get one. In all my studies of Exceptional people, there is one common denominator: they all journaled.

Strategy #4: Recreating Your Thoughts

Purpose:

*Create the thoughts that will lead to your desired results

*Eliminate the thinking that is keeping you from your dreams

*Develop the mindsets needed to change your current circumstances into the ones you want

*Learn the skills for becoming your best self

*Program yourself so you build new productive habits

*Build your strength against naysayers

*Change your self-talk into your best friend

Recreating your thoughts is done by repetition, constantly filling your mind with the right messages, thoughts, and insights. Keep in mind this will take time and consistent effort.

The problem is, we don't really think. Yes, you have thoughts going through your mind always, but you are not choosing them. You are simply letting outside forces, such as the media, others around you, and current circumstances, determine your thoughts. Our internal dialog either builds us or destroys us, and recreating your thoughts means taking control of those messages, deciding what you will or will not allow to enter your mind.

Achieving this strategy is as simple as filling your mind daily, as often as possible, with the input that will help you switch your current thinking into thoughts of confidence. It is said that we are what we think about, so you must recreate your thoughts to think like the person you long to be. Your current thoughts have landed you where you are today, so the only way to change your future is to change the way you think.

Step 1: Fill your mind with inspiring input

All the knowledge and answers you need can be found between the covers of books, yet very few seek the wisdom found in them. Exceptional people take time daily—even if it as little as five minutes—to read because they know it will build their confidence and help them grow and develop.

The best way to look at something from a different angle is to see it through the eyes of others, and that is what books do. You will find many of the same concepts in numerous books on a subject, but each author will have their own twist or way of imparting their thoughts. Some will resonate with you while others will not, and some will make you think in a whole new way.

Anything you want to be or become, someone before you has done, so use this knowledge to create the self you wish to become. You don't have to reinvent the wheel, just adapt it to suit you. Seeking out wisdom and guidance is how you develop your skills, talents, and dreams.

Books are a great way to lose yourself in another world. Not all learning has to come from self-help books; there are many great stories that will help you see things you have never seen. Ayn Rand is one of my favorite storytellers, with insight and wisdom intertwined among the intrigue.

Your library should have a diverse selection because to learn and grow, you must go beyond your norm. Select books about things you like, enjoy, and want to learn about, and books from authors who have traveled the road you wish to pursue. There is no better teacher than experience, so try to learn from those who have gone before you. Choose books that will help you develop the mindsets of the confident—remember confidence is learned and developed, not given.

There are millions of great books full of diamonds and more available every day; you just need to take the time to mine for the hidden gems. I provide a list of some of the books that have helped me develop in the reference section. I suggest you pick one and start building your library today.

Another great way to get all the wisdom from books is through audible books so you can listen while driving or working out (or if you just prefer this method). However, keep in mind that the act of reading provides other skills that listening will not, so try to use both methods.

In addition to books, audio programs are a must. They are designed to teach you new skills and ways of thinking and help you develop yourself. This method is a bit more targeted: you can choose a program that focuses on building the skills you wish to develop. Remember, repetition is the key, so you will not only want to continually build your learning library but also continually revisit it to keep your thoughts sharp.

Read at least one day from your journal every day, looking for the insights from your own thoughts, so you can discover what to build upon or what to work on removing from your life.

Step 2: Change the questions you ask yourself

One of the most common ways to degrade yourself is to ask the wrong questions. Wrong questions are disempowering; they put you in the wrong mindset and are very powerful in directing your internal dialog. Reinventing yourself comes down to asking better questions about yourself, your direction, and your objectives, and being very honest with your answers.

Example:

If you ask yourself*:* "Why can't I lose weight?" you might answer, "Because I have no willpower," or "I have no discipline."

Instead, ask, "What are three things I can do this week to help me get in better shape?"

If you ask, "Why can't I do this?" your answer may be, "Because I'm stupid," or "I don't know how to do this."

Instead, ask, "What skills do I need to develop to do this?"

If you ask, "Why don't I have any money?" you may say, "I'm a loser," or "I don't have a good job."

Instead, ask, "What one thing can I implement this week to get on the road to greater financial success?"

Your questions can create negative thoughts and emotions, and bad questions produce bad answers.

Changing your questions empowers you to brainstorm ways to answer your questions instead of creating more problems. Remember, always work to be a part of the solution, not the problem. Change your questions to ones that provoke you to think of ways to get what you want, not what you want to avoid.

Step 3: Change the way you talk to yourself

If you would step back and listen to the statements you make to yourself, you would be astounded. If someone else spoke to you the way you talk to yourself, you would soon rid them from your life. So you must start paying attention to what you say to yourself.

Example:

Don't say, "I can't get out of this situation, I'm stuck and that is the way life is."

Instead, say, "I can change these circumstances. I do not have to allow my life to go in this direction any longer."

Don't say, "I will never make more money," "I am just happy to get by," or "I could never have a life of riches."

Instead, say, "I am as talented as anyone else. I have been granted the same opportunities as them. I just need to learn the skills, mindsets, and habits they have developed. They started out the same as me and if they can do it, so can I."

Don't say, "I can never be confident, I wasn't born with it, that is just not me."

Instead, say, "Confidence is gained, not given, and all I have to do is follow the strategies, insights, and tips in this book and I will become the confident person I deserve to be."

If your self-talk is full of doubt, how can you be successful? You must learn to be your own cheerleader and best friend.

Step 4: Choose your input wisely

While you are carefully working hard to input the right information in your mind, you will need to be just as careful with the input that will seep in unnoticed. Limit your exposure to negative media of all kinds; unfortunately, the world puts far more emphasis on the negative than the positive. Remind yourself that what the media reports, what others are saying on social media, and the conversations you hear are merely their perspective, which does not make it true. There is a lot of noise in the world and if you are not careful, it can drown out your thoughts by overpowering them. Negative input can go undetected and that is the thing you must be on the lookout for. Choose what you will allow in and who you associate with carefully.

Step 5: Acknowledge your achievements

At the end of the day, write down at least one achievement for the day in your journal on your achievements page. Don't dismiss anything. This is a no-judgment zone. It is about what you feel you accomplished, no one else. It doesn't have to be anything big or earth moving to earn a spot. Taking time just to do this step is an accomplishment, so write it down. If it is the third, fourth, or thirtieth day you have taken the time to do this step, write down the achievement of consistency. Even if you missed a day or two but came right back to this habit, that is a huge achievement because you didn't give up.

Not allowing limiting thoughts or beliefs to derail you keeps you in the right mindset. This is work, but "I'm worth it" deserves a spot daily. Don't worry if it is the same one over and over; this builds momentum and creates a sense of accomplishment and fulfillment. All achievements are necessary on this journey to Bling.

Tools needed:

Books

Audio books

Audio training programs

Achievement pages, found at FromBlahToBling.com

Strategy #5: Creating New Habits

Purpose:

*Build momentum and excitement and give you a feeling of accomplishment

*Change your current results into desired results

*Replace defeating habits with success habits

*Provide a method for tracking progress (achievement is only accomplished by measuring results)

You are your habits, and your habits create and define who you are. If you look around your life, it is a direct result of the habits you have day in and day out. Your habits can be good or bad and it is up to you to decide what you want to be and then structure your habits around that.

Example: Bathing suit models don't drink beer, eat pizza and wings, and lay around the house watching TV or losing themselves in social media. They had to create habits that would provide the results they wanted, such as developing the correct mindsets around the things they would need to do, not looking at them as things they *had* to do. These habits include healthy eating, working out, and getting up early to accomplish all the things necessary before the lights and cameras hit them. They just don't wake up fit, trim, and gorgeous—no, they have adopted habits that get and keep them there.

Creating new habits take time and practice. It would be nice if we could just gain a new habit at the snap of our fingers, but we can't. Habits are actions you take consistently that determine your outcomes, and although you may feel bad habits develop overnight, they don't. They were formed one bad choice at a time and the pattern continued.

Step 1: Review your journal to search for your current habits

There is no better way to discover your limiting habits then to see them in your own words. Go back through your journals, reviewing the patterns you highlighted.

Example: The habit of perfectionism was revealed to me in my journal pages day after day, year after year. I had big plans, promises, and goals, but I always said something like, "I will write my book when I become a better writer," or "I will start my new business once I get everything perfect: the right logo, brand, program." You name it, I was always procrastinating till everything was just right, perfect. I constantly told myself that I was never good enough.

For my first couple of years, I never reviewed my journals. It was when I started going back and reading what I wrote that my habits revealed themselves. I then added the highlighting method, so I could quickly scan my journals to remind me of habits I wanted to replace.

Step 2: Look at your goals

Research the habits needed to accomplish your goals, add them to your action steps, and start consistently doing them today. The brainstorming exercise will help you realize what you need to change so you can achieve your dream instead of giving up on it.

Step 3: List the habits and patterns you have discovered

Make a list of the current habits you have identified you need to rid yourself of. Directly across from each one, write the habit you need to replace it with. When you find yourself wanting to resort back to the defeating habit, don't try to strong-arm yourself into not doing it, simply do the new desired habit. By eliminating an action without replacing it with a new one, you create a void, a space where you do not know what to do. This gives you a plan to fill the gap, so no willpower is needed: you simply do something else.

Example:

Procrastination *instead* Always have action steps prepared

Picking up fast food because you are tired *instead* Plan healthy meals in advance that are quick and easy

Overwhelmed and stressed *instead* Plan your most important tasks, prioritize them

Step 4: Track for success

Once you have identified two or three habits you wish to develop (just like goals, don't overwhelm yourself), post the list beside your wall calendar. Choose a colored marker for each one. Each day that you do your new habit, use the coordinating colored marker to number the day starting with 1. This is a count up to your future success, unlike the normal count*down* method we are used to for an event that ends. You are building a new life one day at a time.

If you skip a day, you must begin again with the number 1 until you have successfully reached the number 30 with no gaps. Habits are created over time, not in a day or a week, and skipping a day gives an opportunity for the old habit to continue. Once you reach 30, you have built a good foundation for the new habit—on to 31!

If you skip a day, you will begin with 31 and continue working toward 60. This gives you a sense of accomplishment and the incentive to keep going. It reminds you that you have done this new habit for at least 30 days, so why not go for 60? Before you know it, this will have become a challenge to better yourself every day. When you review your calendar, it will become your wall of inspiration. It will be a visual of your accomplishments which will provide the motivation to keep going.

When you have successfully reached 90 days with no gaps, you can select new habits to develop because these have now become a part of who you are. No cheating—if you haven't truly done the work, don't give yourself credit. If you give yourself credit when it wasn't truly due, you will only cheat yourself and your future results.

Never forget where you came from. Keep notes in your journal of your journey to new habits, the struggles and challenges and how you overcame them. If at any time you find yourself skipping a daily habit that has gotten you were you want to be, stop and add it back to your calendar. It only takes a few slips to allow the old defeating habits back into your life; it is a very slippery slope unless you always check your footing for secure ground to stand on.

Tools needed:

Year-at-a-glance wall calendar

Colored markers

Dedication

Strategy #6: Caring for Your Health

Purpose:

*Give yourself a healthy body to carry you through life

*Have more energy

*Gain confidence

*Increase self-esteem

*Maintain a good body image

*Achieve mental clarity

One of the biggest misconceptions is that we don't have to care for ourselves, that there is a pill that will take care of whatever it is. That eating healthy is only for those who want to be thin and don't enjoy life. We put eating healthy and exercising at the bottom of the list of priorities. We are just too busy, there are so many things to do, we have to meet this deadline, run the kids here, get groceries, clean the house, go to work, and on and on and on.

We all get one and only one body to carry us through life; we can't trade it in for a new one like our vehicles or homes. Yet we neglect it until one day it breaks down and we have no other choice than to try to fix it. This results in even more lost time, doctor appointments, hospital visits, lost time at work, downtime from sickness, and mental anguish.

We then play catch-up trying to correct all the wrongdoing we have allowed for years. We settle for taking drugs to help cure us, but there is no prescription that will cure you. The only cure is taking care of yourself through proper diet and exercise. The very best prescription for a healthy body is prevention: avoid getting sick in the first place.

The foods you eat affect far more than your weight, even though that may be the first result of poor choices that you notice. However, what you eat determines how you think, how you act, your energy, your confidence, and your overall well-being. These effects are not as obvious, but they are a direct result—however, you blame it on other circumstances. This leads to more bad choices, because you don't truly understand the reasons why you are feeling the way you do.

You think, "I'm tired so I will pick up some fast food tonight," and when you get home, you convince yourself you had a stressful day, so you deserve a glass of wine which makes you even more tired, so you skip exercising. You plant yourself in front of the TV to escape, telling yourself that tomorrow you will do better. The problem is tomorrow will not be any different because your bad choices of today will affect your energy, enthusiasm, thoughts, and mental strength tomorrow as much as today.

You have to realize and accept that in order to break these patterns, you have to start taking better care of the one and only vessel you have been given today. No one will demand it of you; you must demand it of yourself and not settle for what everyone else is doing. Stop feeling sorry for yourself, saying things like "It's not fair," "I deserve this," "Everyone else is doing it." You deserve to be healthy, vibrant, and free, but you can never be free if you are under the control of health issues. Life is short, so decide to get the most of every day. Stop wasting valuable time by settling for less than your best health.

Life is not about constant sacrifice, it is about enjoying everything in moderation. By establishing guidelines for your health, you can have your cake and eat it too, just not every day. Enjoying your favorite adult beverage—I love my wine—is relaxing and fun but must be done in moderation. Exercise is not torture, it is simply moving more; a body in motion stays in motion. Don't become best friends with your couch, TV, or computer; make friends with your sneakers.

Establishing healthy habits is the key to your success. Once they become part of your daily routine, you will start doing them without any thought. Imagine looking in the mirror and feeling proud of what you see, climbing those stairs without gasping for air, not being under the control of doctor's appointments that steal your precious time. Developing habits that make you feel good about yourself is far more rewarding than habits that steal your happiness. It's as simple as replacing an old defeating habit with a conquering one.

Example: Once I had built my confidence, I conquered my self-defeating habits of eating almost effortlessly. I used to stress over how much I could eat, measuring, counting, and weighing my food—how exhausting. My mind was filled with worries about what I couldn't have, parties or events I would skip so I didn't get derailed, Blah. Once I developed the habit of eating for my health, my choices became just that: choices. I made it a habit to plan time to shop for healthy foods and plan meals in advance, so I knew what I was eating no matter what the day threw at me.

Research shows 95% of our cells regenerate every 7-10 years, and many every year, so it is never too late to rebuild your health. The key is to not tear down our health quicker than it can recoup and to keep in mind some cells never regenerate so you need to take care of your health every day. Don't believe the lies that once you have a condition, there is nothing you can do, that you will always have to suffer with it. You may have to manage the symptoms of some conditions but through proper care of yourself you can certainly improve them. You can start today rebuilding your health and establishing defenses for prevention for the future.

Tools needed:

The mindset that your health is first and foremost. It is the most important thing you can have. It is not given and can be taken away.

Books on healthy eating. No quick fixes here, you need good solid guidelines.

Cookbooks with new ideas for healthy cooking.

Strategy # 7: Decide to Stop Settling

Purpose:

*Get what you want out of life

*Rid yourself of the circumstances, thoughts, and results stealing your dreams

*Face the reality of what you are tolerating in your life instead of choosing

*Discover what you do and don't do that is holding you back

Choosing to settle sucks the living confidence right out of you. It steals your peace of mind, passion, joy, and so much more. Settling means allowing yourself to be less than your best. The things you settle for can be so small that they go undetected for so long until one day you realize you have settled for so much that your life isn't at all how you had dreamed it would be. The scariest part is you may not even remember your dreams—or worse yet, don't even have any anymore.

This strategy brings everything out in the open, so you can get to the root of the problem. You cannot go from Blah to Bling until you uncover what you have allowed yourself to settle for. One small acceptance of something you didn't really want but chose to endure anyway led to another; small everyday things led to greater issues. It all counts, it all matters.

This exercise will take some real soul searching and facing some real hard realities. When you settle for circumstances, you give up your power to another force. This usually leads to blaming someone, something, or some condition. Using the excuse "It's not my fault, that is just how it is," must stop right here, right now if you wish to step into your new confident life full of Bling. Blah is settling, accepting less than your best, and the only way to move beyond that is to open your eyes to the reality of your choices.

Step 1: Uncover what you have settled for

In your journal, make a section to write down the things you have settled for. You will want to keep this close to remind you so you don't make the same mistakes again. Brainstorm. Look around your life for the results you currently have but are not happy with.

Example:

Here are some suggestions that might help you:

Job

Home

Financial situation

Relationships, spouse, family, friends, children

Health

Physical shape

Knowledge, education

Car

Goals

Vacations

The list is endless and can be as simple as settling for allowing your own limiting beliefs to hold you back. This step can be very painful because you will have to bring things to the surface that were easier to ignore. No more allowing garbage to clutter your life—it's time to clean house. Once you have cleared the unwanted waste out, you will have room to start anew developing the life you choose.

Step 2: Ask yourself difficult but revealing questions

Part of uncovering what you have allowed to happen in your life is asking probing questions.

Example:

Did I really want this job, or did I just settle for what was the easiest because I didn't believe I could do better?

Do I love my spouse, or did I get married because the clock was ticking, all my friends were getting married, or I was looking for someone to support me?

Am I truly being a good friend, spouse, mother, dad, etc....or am I just getting by instead of giving my best to my relationships?

Is this the car I want or did I just pick what I could afford instead of deciding how I could better myself to earn more to own the vehicle I truly want?

Do I live where I want, or did I settle here because I was afraid to go out into the world?

Am I eating unhealthy food because it is easier than putting in the effort to cook nutritious meals for me and my family?

Do I choose other activities instead of making time to exercise so I am healthy?

Have I dedicated time to further educate myself, so I can better myself or did I give up on that when I graduated?

Do I have goals, or do I just go with the flow, allowing my life to be whatever happens instead of directing it?

For every result in your life, ask yourself, "Is this what I really want, or did I simply choose to accept it?" Be brutally honest here, there is only one judge and jury: you! No one else's opinion matters here, this is you being totally real with yourself. This may be the hardest strategy to do because it requires you to truthfully search your soul, to ask the really tough questions and then answer them with honesty. Facing reality is the only way to move beyond delusion, so don't skip or diminish this one.

Tools needed:

Courage

Honest

Closing Words of Inspiration

I hope you have read this entire book and not just skipped around avoiding some of the chapters because you think you don't need them. The very ones you avoid are probably the ones you need most—you may be avoiding them because they are the hardest to accept or too much work. Allowing yourself to settle for instant satisfaction and avoiding taking responsibility and making difficult changes are probably some of the reasons you purchased this book in the first place. By skipping important steps, challenges, and risks you have robbed yourself of confidence.

A life of confidence is worth every effort, struggle, and pain you might endure. Remind yourself it will be hard, but worth the fight. It really is simple though, if you will just adopt the mindsets, traits, habits, and strategies within this book. All it takes is one small choice, decision, and action at a time.

Don't jump in the waters of change all at once—it takes time. Failing to take baby steps that bridge the gap to the other side will leave you discouraged and drowning in defeating thoughts, and you will settle for the life preserver of average because it's safer, and you will retreat back to the shorelines of Blah.

All you must do is decide to change and become a little better every day. That's it, that is all you have to do. Before you know it, you will become the confident person you long to be.

This book is nothing more than words unless you decide to make the effort to create change in your life. The insights about the traits, habits, and mindsets of others who have gone before you to create the life of their dreams are here to help you do the same. Realizing their struggles helps you see that you are not alone on your journey—there are many others who strive daily to overcome and conquer the same difficulties you do.

If you want to live a life of *Bling,* with over-the-top self-confidence, and actually like the image you see staring back at you in the mirror, then you can't afford to not read every chapter of this book and make it your guide to creating the life you have always dreamed of. You were not created to struggle, to just accept circumstances as they are, and most importantly, to not love and appreciate the wonderful person you are, full of possibilities, talents, and gifts.

This is your guide book. Once you have read the book from start to finish, you can come back whenever you need a refresher, motivation, or inspiration and reread the chapters you need over and over. Remember, not everyone struggles with all of them, but we all have our weaknesses to overcome. The stories will show you how others have learned the secrets to gaining confidence. The sections you need will change from day to day: some days you will struggle with one thing and tomorrow it will be something completely different.

The point is, we all have challenges and struggles; the difference between the successful and the failures is quitting. The secret is to have a go-to plan to help you through the difficult times. All it takes is a reminder, and repetition is key, so make this part of your lifelong commitment to keep yourself confident, moving toward your dreams, and not allowing the grips of past failures to creep back into your new life.

The strategies will work if you will make the commitment to use them. I never promised you victory without challenge. You will be faced with some difficult changes, realizations, and tough decisions. This book is here to guide you, inspire you, and support you, however, as I said before, your motivation must come from within you. It must come from a place inside that says, "No more settling for circumstances or results in my life that I don't want."

The easy way out is to say, "This was all good information, but it will just take too much work, I will just keep on settling." That would be such a tragedy because life is meant to be lived to the hilt. What is the purpose of living if you are not striving for success?

Whether you accept it or not, there is no going back to the person you were before you read this book because you now know the secrets to a confident, successful, happy, and purposeful life. If you choose to remain where you are you will no longer be able to do so in delusion.

You now have the knowledge that things could be different. You now know what needs to be done, so if you choose not to implement these strategies, you will go through life knowing you could have made a change but chose not to. You now have the knowledge that you can live a life of Bling, confidence, and purpose—you are no longer in the dark.

Through the experiences of others who have been in your shoes too shared throughout this book, you can learn how to turn your life into a success just like they did. All you must do is start. Just small simple changes and improvements each day. Make creating your life as you want it a priority; focus on it. Don't leave your future to chance, a glancing thought with no effort. You were put here on this earth to make a difference, for yourself and for others. Believe that you really can, because You Can!

You must stop excusing yourself when you allow Blah into your life. Own it and don't surrender to your weaknesses. Anger is one of the strongest feelings, so get good and mad at yourself, and act. Don't get mad at me for shedding light on the subject; own up to your choices. Decide to slam the door in the face of the old you and open a new door of possibilities that leads to the person you deserve to be. Your life is a direct result of your choices. Like it or not, it is.

It is your responsibility to devote your life to be your best, giving your best, finding the best in others, to improving at least one life in some way. Make the world a little better place by always striving to be your best no matter how small or simple it may be. If you do this, your life will always be a huge success because it is not about what you have, but about what you do with what you have. Success is not about arriving, it is how you choose to live every minute of your life.

Success is a very personal thing that looks different to all of us. It is not a competition. It is not striving to achieve or perform to impress others. It is simply seeking excellence, doing your best based on your skills. Doing things that are fulfilling, heart-warming, and meaningful to you. It is knowing at the end of the day when you lay your head down to rest that you have the satisfaction in your heart you have given your best.

Your time is right now, so decide that you are not going to settle anymore. Starting today, you will begin to build the confident life you have always desired. Confidence is nothing more than feeling good about yourself, and that is accomplished by knowing you have done your best. Small everyday improvements are all achievements that give you fulfillment, and that makes you feel good about yourself.

Go forward with courage and strength. Your Bling awaits you!

References

These are some of the books and programs that has helped me succeed, there are many more and the list continues to grow.

The Bible

The Magic of Believing by Claude M. Bristol

T.N.T. It Rocks the Earth by Claude M Bristol

Secret of the Ages by Robert Collier

The Magic of Thinking Big by David Schwartz

The Power of Positive Thinking by Norman Vincent Peale

The Psychology of Persuasion by Robert B. Cialdini Ph. D

Leadership and Self-Deception by The Arbinger Institute

First Things First by Stephen R. Covey

The 7 Habits of Highly Effective people by Steven R Covey

One Small Step Can Change your Life-The Kaizen Way by Robert Maurer Ph. D

Focal Point by Brian Tracy

Goals by Brian Tracy

Eat That Frog by Brian Tracy

The Science of Getting Rich by Wallace D. Wattles

Think and Grow Rich by Napoleon Hill

Millionaire Success Habits by Dean Graziosi

Atlas Shrugged by Ayn Rand

Fountainhead by Ayn Rand

The Success Principles by Jack Canfield

177 Mental Toughness Secrets of the World Class by Steve Siebold

Die Fat or Get Tough by Steve Siebold

How Rich People Think by Steve Siebold

Choose Yourself by James Altucher

The Compound Effect by Darren Hardy

The Entrepreneur Roller Coaster by Darren Hardy

The War of Art by Steven Pressfield

What is your What by Steve Olsher

Attitude is Everything by Keith Harrell

What's Bugging You by Keith Harrell

The Way to Wealth by Benjamin Franklin

The Richest Man in Babylon by George S. Clason

As a Man Thinketh by James Allen

What to Say when you Talk to Yourself by Shad Helmstetter Ph. D

The Dynamic Laws of Prosperity by Catherine Ponder

Man's search for Meaning by Viktor E. Frankl

Psycho-Cybernetics by Maxwell Maltz M.D.

Bull's Eye by Robert Kennedy

Positivity by Barabara L. Fredickson

The Power of Will by Anthony Parinello

Visioning Lucia Capacchione

When Smart People Fail by Carole Hyatt and Linda Gottleb

Uncommon Friends by James Newton

On Being a Real Person by Harry Emerson Fosdick

The Emotional Revelation by Norman R. Rosenthal M. D.

Waiting for Your Cat to Bark by Bryan & Jeffrey Eisenberg

Selling You by Napoleon Hill

Always Follow your Dreams edited by Susan Polis Schutz

Power VS. Force by David R. Hawkins M.D.

The Rhythm of Life by Matthew Kelly

Handbook to Higher Consciousness by Ken Keyes Jr.

You2 by Price Pritchett Ph. D

The Artist Way buy Julia Cameron

You were Born Rich by Bob Proctor

The Genius in all of Us by David Shenk

Empower your Thoughts by Scott Allan

Outwitting the Devil by Napoleon Hill

The Strangest Secret by Earl Nightingale

How to Stop Worrying and Start Living by Dale Carnegie

How to Win Friends and Influence People by Dale Carnegie

Aristotle: Complete Works

Complete Works of Confucius

In the Buddha's Words

Authors with countless books I like

Everything he wrote Jim Rohn

Orison Swett Marden

Ralph Waldo Emerson

Napoleon Hill

William Walker Atkinson

Og Mandino

Wayne W. Dyer

John Maxwell

James Allen

Robert T. Kiyosaki-Rich Dad

Programs:

Jim Rohn

Bob Proctor

John Wooden- Pyramid of Success

About the Author

Venus Stark strives every day to live a life of purpose, one full of passion, excitement and meaning. Her mission is to empower you to strive to live an Exceptional, Confident life and not accept anything less. She dedicates her life to constant personal and professional development. The driving force of all her success was developed through the insights, wisdom, observations and experiences of many confident successful people. By developing all of that knowledge into proven techniques she has been able mentor countless people in her life, helping them find their passions, gain confidence and become their best, so that they may thrive and flourish.

She has 30+ years of experience in sales and service which requires confidence, persistence and determination. Her wide variety of experiences has provided a huge array of wisdom, perceptions and insights through all the wonderful people she meets along her journey. Her goal is to share the empowering knowledge with others through her writings, products and services all designed to be a guide to put Bling into your life.

Venus currently lives on the Mason-Dixon line in Garrett County Maryland, she loves that she can be in 2 states at the same time and never leave home. She enjoys life with her best friend Jeff, her husband and 3 precious fur babies Tylei Lae, Harley and Mr. Qley, along with family and countless friends. She never wants to retire, instead wants to spend her life making a difference and living with purpose.

Venus@BlahtoBling.com

www.FromBlahtoBling.com

92797080R00135

Made in the USA
Columbia, SC
31 March 2018